Again! Again!

– understanding schemas
in young children

Again! Again!

– understanding schemas in young children

Stella Louis, Clare Beswick,
Liz Magraw, Lisa Hayes

Edited and with additional material by
Sally Featherstone

Reprinted 2008, 2009 (twice), 2010
Published 2008 by A&C Black Publishers Limited
36 Soho Square, London W1D 3QY
www.acblack.com

ISBN 9781905019953

Written by Stella Louis, Clare Beswick, Liz Magraw, Lisa Hayes.

Editing and additional material by Sally Featherstone.

Photographs by Stella Louis, Sally Featherstone, Sarah Featherstone, Kerry Ingham.

Cover drawing by Kerry Ingham.

Printed in Great Britain by Latimer Trend & Company Limited

This book is produced using paper that is made from wood grown in managed, sustainable forests. It is natural, renewablea and recyclable. The logging and manufacturing processes confirm to teh environmental regulations of the country of origin.

To see our full range of titles visit **www.acblack.com**

Preface

Stella Louis is an early years consultant and trainer for the London Borough of Southwark. While working as a nursery nurse in 1991, she attended a lecture on block play by Professor Tina Bruce. It was during this lecture that Stella was introduced to the concept of schemas as a tool to inform planning, provision and observations of babies and young children. Schemas fascinated Stella as she watched her own child, Hannah-Louise, grow explore and develop. In 2002 Stella completed an MA in Early Childhood Education. The introductory sections of this book have been based on Stella's work, whose idea the book was.

Liz Magraw is an experienced teacher who has been head teacher at Merrivale Nursery School, Nottingham since September 2003, where the excellent practice has been recognised by OFSTED who deemed the school to be outstanding. Liz has led this nursery into establishing innovative practice and research and is active in supporting the development of Forest School initiatives locally, regionally and nationally.

Lisa Hayes is a teacher and trainer, who worked as an early years and primary school teacher before specialising in early learning in outdoor environments and Forest Schools. Lisa has been nursery teacher and SENCo at Merrivale since September 2002, and deputy head teacher since 2006. Since joining Merrivale Lisa and Liz have undertaken research projects with Creative partnerships Action Research Awards (CARA) looking at the application of schemas to personalised learning.

Liz and Lisa have written a chapter describing how at Merrivale they have created a system of observing and planning following observations of the schemas children are currently exploring. They include examples of the planners they have devised to support their work with three and four-year-olds at the nursery.

Clare Beswick is an early years writer and trainer, with long experience in working with young children, particularly those under three with special needs, where her specialist knowledge has supported work with children and their families. Clare's recent work has been published in early years magazines, the Baby Book Series, Baby and Beyond, Tough Times and the Little Books. She has worked closely with Stella, Liz and Lisa, to shape the text for Again! Again! and has researched and identified the resources and equipment that practitioners might provide to support schema play.

Sally Featherstone is a consultant, trainer and writer with a long-standing and continuing interest in children's learning. She has had the pleasure of editing and in some cases adding a few words to the text of this book.

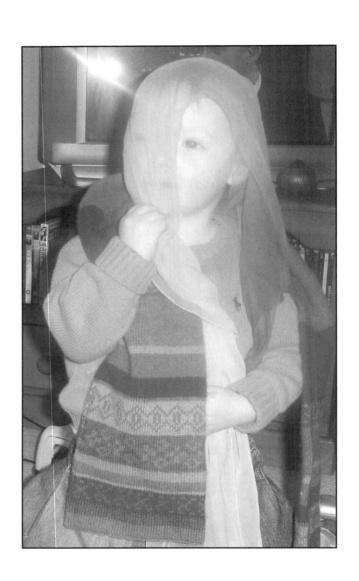

Contents

Introduction

This book is an introduction to schema play in young children, and its main intention is to help early years practitioners identify and understand what schemas are, why children get involved in schema play, and how they can plan for and support children's learning, using knowledge of the schemas they are currently exploring. Practitioners working with the Early Years Foundation Stage (EYFS), students studying child development, parent development workers and early years trainers and managers may also benefit from revisiting its contents.

Much work has already been done in recognising and valuing the process of learning through play, and many great thinkers in the field of early childhood development have explored the repetitive play patterns which engage children as they turn their experiences into knowledge of the world and skill in making sense of it. This volume is intended to support practitioners as they grapple with the tensions of following an externally imposed curriculum that emphasises moving on, while securing the needs of individual children for whom repetition is an essential part of learning.

Readers will find an overview of the **theory** behind the concept of schemas, its influence on good practice in early years provision, and some of the research which has informed our current thinking. This historical perspective is linked to the place of schemas in the Practitioner Guidance for the EYFS.

Examples of the most frequently observed schemas are included, with illustrations and descriptions of each, along with suggestions for resources and ways of using your observations of schemas to help with your planning.

Eight schemas are defined and discussed in detail in the section 'Schemas and Play'. These are:

> **Trajectory**
> **Orientation**
> **Connecting**
> **Rotation**
> **Enclosing**
> **Enveloping**
> **Positioning**
> **Transporting.**

The book also examines schema clusters, and how practitioners can take advantage of recognising them to assist with children's development.

Examples of the schemas are illustrated by the use of **observations** of babies and young children, made by practitioners as they witness the schemas in action. The significance and importance of symbolic play and how young children present their thoughts, ideas and feelings through spontaneous, self-initiated interactions and experiences are featured throughout this book.

The **resource pages** focus on the underlying repeated patterns running through children's play, based on the eight identified schemas. Practitioner observations accompany the text, with assessments of what children are learning and how they are developing. These pages provide practitioners with professional advice on engaging with children's schemas and providing appropriately challenging activities across the range of learning experiences recommended in the Guidance for the EYFS.

The section entitled '**Look, listen and note**' focuses on the role of the practitioner in observing and recording children's development and learning, and tips are provided about what to watch out for in accordance with the broad stages of development as described in the EYFS. Practitioners can also learn how to use their observations to build up an accurate picture of a child's achievements and progress, and how to share these with the child and their parents.

The chapter '**Using observations of schemas in planning**' describes how one nursery setting has built schema play into their observations and planning for individuals and groups of children. The process is described, and examples of planning are included.

'**Working with other practitioners and settings**' provides practical information on how to explain schemas to parents and other practitioners in the various settings children may attend, and describes strategies for engaging parents as partners and co-researchers in identifying and understanding schematic behaviour.

What is a schema?

The word 'schema' is generally used to describe patterns of repeated behaviour which children use to explore and express their developing ideas and thoughts through play and exploration. This section explores what schemas are, and how they contribute to children's learning.

Babies and young children can often be observed repeating actions, for example, dropping things from their highchair, cot or buggy, again and again. This repeated action helps the child to establish internal cognitive structures (schemas) in the brain. Schemas help young children to construct meaning in what they are doing, and observing schemas in children's play provides practitioners with insight into the ideas and concepts children are currently exploring.

'Action alone is not sufficient for learning. To understand their immediate world children must interact thoughtfully with it.'   David Weikart

In September 2008, the Early Years Foundation Stage (EYFS) provided the first single, integrated framework for children from birth to five. The EYFS emphasises the significance of play and schemas in babies' and young children's learning and development. The hands-on, play-based philosophy of the EYFS is rooted in the combined outcomes of educational theory and evidence-based research, where babies and young children are seen as active learners, learning through play.

'As they move around, exploring their ideas babies and toddlers can be observed to be frequently exploring a particular pattern of thought and movement such as in and out, transporting or rotation, exhibiting an underlying logic in their play. Play that appears idiosyncratic or even mischievous can also give clues to children's schematic preoccupations.'
Julia Manning-Morton and Maggie Thorp

Children are constantly engaged in trying to make sense of their world and through play, exploration and repeated schematic play patterns, they are able to integrate their existing knowledge, understanding and experiences, into new situations. Babies and young children learn best in this way from first-hand experiences, when they are able to solve problems, make mistakes, decisions and choices, based on what they already know.

It is important to recognise that children do not do this in a random or haphazard manner. Babies and young children are methodical, systematic and logical as they gather information through their senses and movement, and as they interact with people, objects and the environment. Knowledge and understanding of schemas enables practitioners to support and challenge children's thinking, their ideas and their developing concepts. As practitioners recognise and acknowledge schematic play patterns they can tune into the child's thinking processes, enabling them to develop a genuine interest in what children are doing, offer support, clarify ideas and ask open questions.

The EYFS offers early years practitioners an important and significant definition of schemas;

> *'Schemas are patterns of repeated behaviour in children. Children often have a very strong drive to repeat actions such as moving things from one place to another, covering things up and putting things into containers, or moving in circles or throwing things. These patterns can often be observed running through their play and may vary between one child and another. If practitioners build on these interests, powerful learning can take place.'*
>
> *EYFS Glossary*

Schemas are biological - we are born with the ability and desire to use and construct them, and they are central to young children's learning and development. Babies and young children's schemas are influenced by their genes and their experiences of people and objects. A 17-month-old baby may use a reflex to grasp a slippery object such as an ice cube. But with each new experience of ice the baby's mental map and cognitive structure is refined and changed, becoming more intentional, skilled and informed as the action is repeated. What the baby knows about handling the ice cube becomes better known each time the schema is revisited.

> *'Probably the most important accommodations, or steps forward in knowledge, are where there is a new co-ordination between two separate aspects of knowing.'*
> *Chris Athey*

Schemas are also socio-cultural. Learning and development are influenced by the people we interact with, our experiences in early life, our environment, cultures and codes of conduct, as well as our individual growth and physical development.

> *'How a brain develops hinges on a complex interplay between the genes you're born with and the experiences you have.'*
> *Rima Shore*

Schemas can be seen in children's explorations and interactions with the world, although they may not be consistently displayed or used. A child may abandon a schema, revisit a previous one, or go for some time without displaying any schema behaviour. Children may use schemas to guide them in their questioning, predicting, imagining and speculating as they encounter new challenges, experiences, resources and materials. Schemas can change over time, becoming more complex and sophisticated, and children may be involved with more than one schema at a time.

Many different schemas have been identified and described, and this list represents some of the most common types seen in children's play and exploration:

Trajectory: an interest in dropping things from a highchair or cot or climbing up and jumping off things.

Rotation: a fascination with spinning, including wheeled toys, being swung round or riding on a roundabout.

Enclosing: putting borders around drawing and paintings, making block enclosures, for example, animals in a field with fences around them.

Enveloping: completely covering themselves or objects, wrapping things up, putting objects into bags.

Transporting: moving themselves or objects from one place to another, bringing objects to an adult, carrying things round in bags and containers.

Connecting: joining and disconnecting train tracks, using construction sets, gluing or taping materials together.

Positioning: An interest in lining up objects such as cars, books or shoes, or organising them in groups.

Orientation: an interest in putting objects or their own bodies in different places and positions - upside down, on their side.

Schemas may change over time, as with time and experience they become more and more sophisticated.

'As babies move and play, they experience movement, sound, texture, light and pattern, taste and smell. These sensory-motor experiences become mental operations called schemas. Schemas become more complex as the child assimilates experiences into their existing schemas and also adjusts their existing schemas to accommodate new experiences.'

Julia Manning-Morton and Maggie Thorp

Children may also use schemas to help them deal with their feelings and emotions, and children interested in a similar schema may be observed playing together. They may also use different schemas in different settings and at home.

'David and Saul used the climbing frame, walking up the slide, turning and running down, then later using the steps to ascend and descending by way of the slide.'

Cathy Nutbrown

What is a schema?

Observing schemas gives practitioners an additional way of considering a child's development alongside indications of their current interests, and this allows practitioners to offer appropriate activities and experiences at just the right time, enabling them to explore their concerns in as many ways as possible until they are satisfied that their learning is secure.

Understanding schemas helps practitioners to:

- find out more about how babies and young children learn;
- observe and recognise individual children's current schemas;
- plan appropriately to support schemas;
- build on babies' and young children's preferred way of learning;
- support and challenge children's thinking.

The relationship between play, development and schemas is not by any means incidental, and schemas are central to young children's learning. The way in which babies and young children are driven by their schemas in their play is too powerful and purposeful for practitioners to ignore.

References

Piaget, Jean. (1969) The Mechanisms of Perception; Routledge & Kegan Paul

Meade, A. One Hundred Billion Neurons: How do they become organised? Advances in Applied Early Childhood Education. Vol. 1. Promoting Evidence-base Practice in Early Childhood Education: Research and its Implications; JAL

Weikart, D. (2001) Early Childhood Education: Need and Opportunity; Unesco

Manning-Morton, J. and Thorp, M. (2003) Key Times for Play; The First Three Years; Open University Press

Early Years Foundation Stage (2006) Consultation; DfES

Athey, C. (1990) Extending Thoughts in Young Children; A Parent-Teacher Partnership; Paul Chapman

Shore, Rima. (1997) Rethinking the Brain, New insights into Early Development; Families and Work Institute

Nutbrown, Cathy. (1999) Threads of Thinking: Young children's learning and the role of the educator; Paul Chapman

Schemas - the theory

Schemas have now been recognised as such an important part of children's growth and learning, that understanding the theory behind schema development is a key responsibility for every early years practitioner. In this part of the book you can gain insight into how schemas have been researched and re-defined to become an integral part of the *Early Years Foundation Stage Framework*.

Long before theory on schemas had been established, early childhood pioneers such as Fredrick Froebel, Rudolph Steiner, Margaret Macmillan, Susan Isaacs and Maria Montessori had all recognised the significance of schema-type behaviour in children's development, learning and play.

In this section we take a historical look at eight of the most influential voices in the development of schemas and the dates of the work they undertook in researching schemas and play.

'Theories help us to predict and to anticipate how children might behave and react. They help us to structure what we observe. Theories help us to make sense of what we see ... When we analyse play, we find ourselves linking what we have found with what other people (theorist) have found. We may find that our observation fits with theories. We may find that they do not. This will help us think deeply ...'
Tina Bruce

Jean Piaget (1896-1980)

'Schemas of action (are) co-ordinated systems of movement and perceptions, which constitute any elementary behaviour capable of being repeated and applied to new situations, e.g., grasping, moving, shaking an object.'

Jean Piaget

Piaget, a Swiss biologist, was among the first to recognise organised behaviour patterns in children under the age of five years. The concept of cognitive structures is central to his theories of learning, and he called this kind of behaviour 'Scheme of thought' or 'Schemas of action'.

Piaget's interest was twofold. He was concerned with the sequence of child development as well as the development and growth of knowledge itself.

He identified four distinct stages of development,

The sensori-motor stage, 0-18 months,

The pre-operational stage, 18 months-7 years

The concrete operational stage, 7 years-12 years

The formal operational stage, 12 years-adulthood

Piaget defined schemas as cognitive structures or mental maps functioning at four levels, for which he outlined several principles. During all four developmental stages the child experiences the environment, using and building on the cognitive structures they have built so far. The new experience either fits easily into the child's cognitive structures so he maintains 'equilibrium', or if the experience is different or new, the child alters their cognitive structures to accommodate the experience. Piaget called this 'stage level theory' and related it to the four developmental stages.

Level 1. The sensori-motor stage, when babies and young children explore and experience the world through their senses, interactions and movement.

Level 2. This stage is sub-divided into symbolic and language development.

Symbolic development, where young children use one thing to stand for another; for instance, a box becomes a house or car. Children are no longer dependent on having real objects to explore.

Language development, children will continue to use familiar sounds and words, and they will start to structure language and make language work for them, using appropriate vocabulary to support their thinking and actions.

Level 3. Function dependency, understanding cause and effect; for example - 'What will happen if I jump in the puddle?'

Level 4. The development of thought, children use logic, reasoning and prior knowledge in their interaction with people, experiences and materials.

Piaget's work on schema theory provided a basis for understanding child development. He believed that children were active learners and that knowledge is not merely transmitted, but must be constructed and re-constructed by the learner. His thinking about child development continues to be influential in early education.

Lev Vygotsky (1896-1934)

Vygotsky was a Russian psychologist, well known during his life in his own country, but whose work was relatively unknown in the west until the 1960s, 30 years after his death. Vygotsky's theories on language and thought were developed at the same time as Piaget's stage level theory. According to Vygotsky, the origins of thought and language have different roots. He proposed that, particularly during early childhood, thought was non-verbal and language was non-intellectual, and that their development lines are not parallel, they cross over again and again. He suggested that at around the age of two, the curves of development of thought and speech, until then separate, meet and join to initiate a new form of behaviour.

Both Piaget and Vygotsky started with the same basic views of the child as a biological organism. However, Vygotsky believed strongly that culture and social interaction contribute to the biological learning process, and he proposed that cultural and social aspects might cause important revisions in children's thinking. Vygotsky believed that once children begin to use one thing to stand for another, they begin to understand the symbolic function of language:

'A child's speech is as important as the role of action in attaining goals. Children not only speak about what they are doing; their speech and action are part of the same complex psychological function, directed towards the solution of the problem at hand.'
                                                                            Lev Vygotsky

Vygotsky recognised that:

> Knowledge is passed from one person to another. He saw **the child as part of both a society and a culture**;

> Interactions and traditions can only be understood **in context** of, or with reference, to these same cultural and historical contexts;

> Knowledge of **what the child can already do** should always be the starting point for further development.

He also underlined the key role of the adult in children's development:

> in **scaffolding children's learning**; and

> in becoming **attuned to what the child already knows, in order to support and extend learning**.

Vygotsky identified the **zone of proximal development** as the difference between the child's capacity to solve problems independently and the capacity to solve problems with assistance from an adult. This description of the role of the adult continues to influence thought and practice today.

For Vygotsky, children's learning was shaped by their cultural and social influences and interactions, and in doing so he identified a significant gap in Piaget's theory. He recognised that learning was a social **and** cultural experience. Learning is linked to physical and cognitive development, but development is not necessarily dependant on learning, and can be furthered by effective interaction with others.

Chris Athey, working in 1972

Chris Athey's work followed the theories and practice of Freidrich Froebel (1782-1852), an early years educator, who died more than a century ago. He pioneered a new approach to working with children, based on the belief that young children are intrinsically motivated and that they learn best through active play, which is deeply significant and important for them to experience first hand.

Chris Athey, a teacher and researcher at a Froebel inspired nursery school built on the theories of Piaget and Vygotsky. Piaget first identified schemas, but Athey was the first to pioneer observations of schemas in a nursery setting. Athey used observations structured on Piaget's stage level theory to make a detailed study of how young children acquire knowledge.

The research project began in 1972, lasted for five years, and was the first of its kind in the United Kingdom. The aim of the project was to 'search for schemas' by following the development of each child's thinking, in collaboration with parents and professionals, and her research findings were presented in 1990 in her book *Extending Thoughts In Young Children; A Parent-Teacher Partnership*.

During the research Chris Athey and her team analysed more than 5000 observations of 20 two- to five-year-olds over a two year period, as they attended three-hour morning sessions at the Froebel Institute Kindergarten. The children involved were described as being from stable but deprived backgrounds.

Interpretations of observations were based on Piaget's notion of cognitive structures (described as schemas), and the findings of the project gave support to Piaget's stage level theory, revealing links to speech, comprehension and prominent schemas.

The definition of a schema used by Chris Athey is:

> *'A schema is a pattern of repeated behaviour into which experiences are assimilated and gradually co-ordinated. Co-ordinations lead to a higher and more powerful schema.'*
> *Chris Athey*

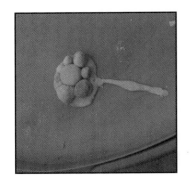

Again! Again!

In her book *Extending Thoughts in Young Children* Chris Athey identified and described ten **graphic schemas**, eleven **space schemas** and nine **dynamic schemas** at varying levels, as well as some of the clusters of schemas:

Graphic schemas	*Space schemas*	*Dynamic schemas*
· Dabs	· Enclosure	· Dynamic vertical schema
· Circles	· Separation & connection	· Back and forth or side to side
· Horizontal lines	· Lines	· Circular direction and rotation
· Vertical lines	· Horizontal, vertical & circular scribbles	· Going over, under or top of
· Downward curves	· Horizontal & vertical co-ordinates, grids & grid orders	· Going round a boundary
· Upward curves		· Containing & enveloping
· Rectangular	· Straight & oblique lines	· Going through a boundary
· Circular enclosures	· Circles & enclosed curves	· Thought internalised action
· Enclosures with radials attached	· Core & radials	· Thought telling a story
· Enclosures with order marks within	· Open & closed arcs	
	· Open continuous triangle (zig-zag)	
	· Angles, triangles & quadrilaterals	

Tina Bruce, working during the 1970s

Tina Bruce, a Froebel-trained teacher, worked on the Froebel Kindergarten project in the 1970's with her fellow teacher and researcher, Chris Athey. When Tina Bruce observed her own children she found that schemas appeared much earlier than was observed in the project children, and this resulted in further research when she became the Director of the Centre for Early Childhood Studies at the Froebel Institute. In 1987-1990 she directed the *Froebel Block Play Project*, working with her research assistant Pat Gura.

Tina Bruce was also influenced by the work of Freidrich Froebel and she fully embraced the Froebelian philosophy that children learn through play, believing that play was important and deeply significant for the development and coordination of schemas. She describes three levels in which schemas operate:

Sensori-motor (learning through the senses and movement)

Symbolic representation (learning through pretend play)

Functional dependency (exploring cause and effect).

However, like Froebel, Tina Bruce did not believe that play for young children should be unstructured. Importance was placed on the role of the adult and on the learning environment when supporting young children to make meaning of their play. For Tina Bruce play is too important to be left to chance, and the aim of the block play project was to support children's play using materials which would offer them cognitive challenge to support thinking and existing schemas.

Five schools were involved in the research, all of which were committed to the principles of Froebel, and where practitioners were already knowledgeable about schemas. Tina Bruce believed that carefully structured and well planned block play gave children the opportunity to collaborate, negotiate, solve problems and co-operate, so unit blocks and hollow blocks were introduced as an integral part of the whole curriculum for children aged three to six years.

The findings of the project confirmed that children explore the world in consistent ways, using unit blocks and hollow blocks to combine horizontal lines and simple verticals, mixing and matching as well as creating more complex structures, both symmetrical and asymmetrical.

Tina Bruce defined a schema as:

'A schema is a repeatable pattern of organisational behaviour which the child generalises, e.g. the trajectory (banging, jumping, climbing up and down, throwing etc).'
                                                                    Tina Bruce

Again! Again!

The block play project identified eight combinations of ways in which children played with blocks to reflect and to support their existing schemas:

Horizontal lines	Intersections and partitions
Simple verticals	Grids
Round and linear enclosures	Central core with radials
Edge ordering and filling in	Arches and zigzags

Cathy Nutbrown, working in 1999

Cathy Nutbrown is a lecturer in Early Childhood Education at the University of Sheffield. She has long experience of working with young children and their parents, and has been a nursery class teacher, researcher, writer and consultant. Her research links young children's schemas directly with their talk, action, representation and thinking. In her book *Threads of Thinking*, she built on the work of Piaget, Vygotsky, Athey and Bruce. Cathy Nutbrown collected observations of children over a ten-year period, drawing on observations in early years group settings where she worked and from children in action at home.

Her aim was to examine:

thought internalising action, where children demonstrate their knowledge and understanding in what they do; for example playing peek-a-boo, singing a song, drawing, building;

thought telling a story, where children create a story to represent their knowledge and understanding, based on a first hand experience.

Cathy Nutbrown linked language and thought to children's repeated patterns of behaviours (their schemas), by observing what children know and understand, what they say and the marks they make. When she analysed her observations, she found that:

- children interested in the dynamic vertical schema would express ideas which related to height, length, division of space, symmetry, mapping, lines and grids;
- children interested in the dynamic circular schema would understand the concept of 'round or circle', would represent circles in their mark making and talk about spinning, getting dizzy, stirring etc;
- in their story telling, children's individual schemas helped them represent a thought, experience or idea;

• many of the children's schemas had mathematical or scientific roots.

She examined the appropriateness of the early years curriculum of the time, (*The Desirable Outcomes of Nursery Education*. HMSO, 1996) in supporting children's learning and development, and believed that play should be at the heart of the early years curriculum, as play underpins the process of learning.

Cathy Nutbrown defined schemas in the following way:

'Early patterns of behaviour seen in babies become more complex and more numerous, eventually becoming grouped together so that babies and young children do not perform single isolated behaviours but co-ordinate their action. Toddlers work hard, collecting a pile of objects in the lap of their carer, walking to and fro, backwards and forwards, bringing one object at a time. They are working on a pattern of behaviour which has a consistent thread running through it.'   *Cathy Nutbrown*

Cathy Nutbrown also introduced a number of principles for partnership working with parents, which recognised parents' crucial role as primary carers and educators of their children. These include:

the importance of consistency, continuity and progression;

the need for equality of opportunity;

working in the interest of the child;

respect and 'the loving use of power'.

This last principle recognised that parents and practitioners are powerful people in a child's life, both groups contributing to the child's learning, so it is crucial that they recognise their power and make 'loving use' of it to ensure that they work in partnership.

PEEP: The Effects of the Peers Early Education Partnership on Children's Developmental Progress

PEEP builds on the work of both Chris Athey and Cathy Nutbrown in developing effective partnerships with parents to help them understand and support their children's learning. Between 1998-2000 the first PEEP project was developed in areas of social deprivation in Oxfordshire.

The aim of the study project was to track children's development, and children aged three years and their parents from five playgroups were chosen from comparable neighbourhoods. The families were divided into two groups - an intervention group and a comparison (control) group, and the parents from the intervention group had weekly meetings with practitioners who openly shared their knowledge of how children learn. The practitioners responded to and valued parent's contributions, insights and knowledge of their children, and offered them support and training in a parents' course during the 33 week programme. The programme focused on helping parents to engage and interact with their children at home, understand the patterns of play, and model how to support and extend learning. The parents from the comparison group had no intervention from practitioners or while attending the pre-school setting with their children.

The findings show that where there was intervention children made significant progress in their learning, when compared with children whose parents did not take part. The study revealed that the children from the intervention group displayed increased levels of confidence and self esteem in their intellectual, cognitive and physical competence, particularly in understanding and expressing language, understanding about books and print, and developing number concepts.

'Children often have favourite ways of playing. Sometimes they seem to need to do things in the same way again and again. Underlying the ways in which they play are their schemas ... the 'mental framework' of children's thinking.' PEEP

The findings of the PEEP project have informed many local and national initiatives to support parents in raising outcomes for children under five.

The Birth to Three Matters Framework 2003

In 2001 the government commissioned Manchester Metropolitan University to produce the *Birth to Three Matters Framework*, aimed at ensuring consistent, high quality provision across the whole sector. Lesley Abbot led a team of early years professionals through a year long development project which involved working with children, parents, practitioners from all parts of the sector, early childhood experts, policy makers and researchers.

The starting point for the project was to build on what was already known about how babies and young children learn, as well as to review evidence-based research literature on early childhood education. The resulting *Birth to Three Matters* pack was distributed throughout the sector, to all practitioners, and was supported by an extensive training programme. The pack included guidance cards, a CD-ROM of examples of good practice, and a video, and the aim of the pack was to provide support, information and guidance for practitioners with responsibility for the care and education of babies and young children under three. *Birth to Three Matters* was underpinned by ten clear principles, and identified four broad stages of development across four aspects of learning and development.

The *Birth to Three Matters* materials made clear the vital importance of relationships in supporting babies' and young children's learning and development, and highlit the role of effective practitioners in extending learning. Babies and young children's repeated play patterns (schemas) are acknowledged in both the practice cards and the video examples as central to their learning and development.

The philosophy and content of the *Birth to Three Matters Framework* were influenced by the thinking of Piaget and Vygotsky, as well as the evidence-based research findings of Athey, Bruce, Gura, Nutbrown, Manning-Morton, Thorp, and the PEEP Project.

> *'Play seems to help lay down implicit memories of skills, dispositions and schemas.'*   Birth to Three Matters, Literature Review

The influence of new research in brain development

The *Birth to Three Matters Framework* also included information on advances in medical technology which have enabled researchers to make new discoveries about young brains.

The work of Rima Shore, described in her book *Rethinking the Brain*, challenges much of the previous understanding of early brain development. Shore believes that genetics, early interaction and first experiences all influence the development of the brain, and this is particularly powerful in children under three. Other recent studies of the workings of young brains provide further insight.

Anne Meade, in her work *One Hundred Billion Neurons; How do they become organised?* considered the relationship between play and brain development. Her study found that play also gives children vital opportunities to lay down schemas.

The findings of Alison Gopnik, Andrew Meltzoff and Patricia Kuhl in their book, *How Babies Think*, were influential in the construction of the Birth to Three pack, and Gopnik's earlier work, explored in her book *Words and Plans: Early Language and the Development of Intelligent Action*, although influenced by Piaget, demonstrates that at birth babies arrive knowing far more than was previously recognised. Gopnik observed language development in children aged one and two years, and when she analysed her observations they clearly illustrated that children use *and* understand words like 'up' and 'down' if they are exploring them within the framework of a trajectory schema. She strongly believed that the action is as important for the child as the word, and her work was incorporated in *Birth to Three Matters* within two aspects (A Skilful Communicator; A Competent Learner).

Again! Again!

For Alison Gopnik a plan, or schema is an action or a series of repeated actions:

'Children and scientists are the best learners in the world, and they both seem to operate in very similar, even identical ways, ways that are unlike even our best computers. They never start from scratch; instead, they modify and change what they already know to gain new knowledge.' Alison Gopnik

This neat re-wording of Piaget's notion of accommodation, assimilation and adaptation, clearly describes a schema.

The Early Years Foundation Stage (EYFS) 2008

The EYFS is the single quality framework to support children from birth to five years. The EYFS builds on key outcomes of recent research, particularly of:

Peers Early Education Partnership (PEEP)

Effective Provision of Pre-school Education (EPPE)

Researching Effective Pedagogy in the Early Years (REPEY)

Brain Research for ECEC Professionals

and on existing documents, including:

The National Day Care Standards

The Curriculum Guidance for the Foundation Stage

The Birth to Three Matters Framework

Every Child Matters.

From September 2008 existing documentation remains as guidance when the EYFS becomes a statutory requirement for settings receiving government funding for provision of out-of-home care for children under five.

The EYFS highlights four themes:

A Unique Child

Positive Relationships

Enabling Environments

Learning and Development

Active learning, play and exploration, creativity and critical thinking are as central to the EYFS as they are to the development of schemas as actions or schemas as thought. Within the EYFS pack there are many references to these key features of experience which help babies and young children make crucial connections in their thinking, and the guidance reiterates the work of Alison Gopnik, recognising that children transform their understanding by behaving like scientists, testing out ideas and experimenting.

'For example, children may need to run, jump and walk through puddles many times to check out what happens. In this way they begin to understand more about the effects of force on water.'　　　　　　　　　*EYFS*

The importance of adult support is emphasised by the focus on sustaining shared thinking, which is highlighted as a means of providing children with appropriate cognitive challenge. Sustained shared thinking, first identified as a key element in successful early years practice in the Effective Practice in Pre-School Environments (EPPE) research, happens when two or more children are deeply engaged in an activity or experience 'with the support of an adult or peer partner', in which they are required to use reason, logic or solve a problem together. Sustained shared thinking describes children when they are engrossed in what they are doing, apply the knowledge they already have and extend it with new discoveries and ways of doing things. The role of the practitioner in recognising, supporting, extending and sustaining children's thinking is emphasised throughout the guidance. *'When children have opportunities to play with ideas in different situations and with a variety of resources, they discover connections and come to a new and better understanding and way of doing things. Adult support in this process enhances their ability to think critically and ask questions.' EYFS*

The development of schemas is embedded throughout the *EYFS Framework*, and the guidance underlines the importance of repeated play patterns in helping babies and young children to transform their understanding of the world around them. The EYFS recognises the need for practitioners to build on children's schematic play patterns. There is agreement that supporting young children in laying secure foundations for learning can sometimes be a long and repetitive process, but knowledge and understanding of schemas will enable practitioners to make sense of what they see when they are observing, assessing and planning for babies and young children.

References

Athey, C. (1990) <u>Extending Thoughts in Young Children</u>; Paul Chapman

Bruce, T. (2001) <u>Learning Through Play</u>; Hodder and Stoughton

Piaget, Jean. (1962) <u>Play, Dreams and Imitations in Childhood</u>; Routledge & Kegan Paul

Vygotsky, L. (1986) <u>Thought and Language</u>; MIT Press

Bruce, T. (1991) <u>A Time to Play</u>; Hodder & Stoughton

Nutbrown, C. (1999) <u>Threads of Thinking</u>; Paul Chapman

Evangelou, M and Sylva, K (2003) <u>PEEP; The Effects of the Early Education Partnership on Children's Developmental Progress</u>; Research Report No 489

Gopnik, A. (1984) <u>Words and Plan</u>; Journal of Child Language Development

<u>Birth to Three Matters: A Review of Literature</u>; DfES, Report no 444

DCSF. (2007/2008) <u>Early Years Foundation Stage</u>

The development of schemas in children's play and learning

This section explores individual schemas and the way they emerge in children's development. Of course, different children will display schemas at different ages and stages, and some may not appear to become 'hooked' on schemas at all.

The trajectory schema

One of the earliest schemas seen in babies is the trajectory schema. This schema is essentially about movement, and it can be seen in babies' actions as they learn to focus on things that move. Even newborn babies can gaze and track, following moving objects with their eyes and sometimes by turning their heads.

In the trajectory schema, patterns of movement emerge in which babies and very young children move their arms, legs and bodies in horizontal and vertical lines, pushing and kicking (horizontal trajectory) or when they drop things or put things in and out of containers such as posting boxes (vertical trajectory).

It is important to recognise that a baby's early experiences and interaction will involve them in a lot of straight line movements. For example, being picked up and put down, being pushed in a buggy or pram; driven in a car or carried on a bicycle, being lifted in and out of a bath or car seat.

The trajectory schema often develops into exploration of straight lines, either up and down or horizontal, and young babies may be observed repeatedly reaching out for objects and placing them in their mouths, kicking their legs, opening and closing their hands, waving their arms up and down or side to side, throwing, pulling and pushing, pointing, rocking, climbing and stepping up and down.

First hand experiences are vital to the exploration of trajectory, as they enable babies to explore and manipulate objects. Babies will use their schematic actions constantly in everything they do, for example as they struggle with new experiences of grasping, throwing, dropping or squeezing. The repeated and repeating nature of the movement is an indication of schema behaviour.

Again! Again!

From the age of about six months babies are attracted to the cause and effect of the toys and objects which they are exploring. For example, a baby will repeatedly squeeze a teddy tightly to make it squeak, push buttons on an activity centre, or put objects in and take them out of buckets and containers. Babies and young children love familiar objects and toys, which require repeated actions to achieve an expected response.

As the trajectory schema develops, babies may start to explore concepts of height and distance. This repeated behaviour is not intended to irritate practitioners or parents; babies are exploring height, length, distance, cause and effect. For example, some babies like to clutch and then let go of toys repeatedly, often dropping them and wanting an adult to fetch them back! Young babies may be observed exploring vertical and horizontal trajectories when they build towers and knock them down, drop things from high chairs or tables, hit or swipe out with their hands and arms, stretching, waving and reaching.

Young children also love to make things move through the air by throwing, jumping, swinging and trailing them, continuing their explorations of trajectory actions and consolidating their knowledge of how objects move.

Later, some children may begin to explore space, shapes and grids in drawing and mark making. They use their knowledge of horizontal and vertical lines to make a connection between open and closed lines, curves and corners. They discover shapes like squares, rectangles and triangles, and they begin to coordinate lines and where they intersect, form crosses, grids, ladders and other patterns.

Practitioners can help children to extend their trajectory schemas by providing appropriate materials and opportunities to explore. For example, if a child has an interest in throwing objects, practitioners could provide a variety of safe projectiles and places to throw them against, into, on, up, over, through. Some children may need frequent opportunities to run and chase each other, building on what they have already assimilated into their thinking, others may become interested in things that move in a straight line such as aeroplanes and birds.

The rotation schema

The rotation schema is seen in children's actions when they turn and rotate objects or themselves. Children may roll their bodies, and are interested in playing with toys and simple everyday objects that spin, twist or turn. The rotation schema can be very dynamic and energetic, as children run or spin in circles, ride round and round on bikes, twist and spin objects and toys, ribbons, scarves and ropes, and love being spun round and round by adults.

This pattern of play links things that turn with turning themselves, and some children become fascinated with turning and spinning toys.

Jack aged two, shows his childminder how he can spin a globe round and round in the same direction on its stand, at the same time describing to her what he is doing.

Nicholas aged four, is observed playing with a helicopter he has made from Lego. Pointing to its propellers he says, 'When this goes round my helicopter goes up, up in the sky, moon and stars'.

Children will also ask questions about the functions of the turning and spinning objects they are interested in, and this is an opening for practitioners to tune into what children already know about rotation and for them to gain a deeper understanding of the ideas children are currently exploring. Understanding the rotation schema can help adults to recognise and understand the sometimes puzzling or even annoying repeated patterns that run through children's play.

With support and help from parents and practitioners, children's early experiences are assimilated and gradually coordinated into secure understanding about rotation.

The enclosing schema

The enclosure schema is often observed in children's actions once they have explored vertical and horizontal lines through a trajectory schema. Interest in enclosures may begin in early experience of being in a variety of enclosed spaces, for example, their cot and playpen, buggy or highchair.

Children may begin to join lines or build structures with materials and resources of all kinds to form enclosures. Some have an interest in representing round enclosures, others create square or rectangular enclosures or explore structures as a pattern emerges in actions that link the enclosing of spaces, objects and themselves. Children may do this by building fences or walls, or by carefully filling in spaces they have constructed. They may also put borders round their drawings or creations. Some children fill their enclosures in an ordered way, for example by adding toy animals in fields or farmyards. Other children may prefer to lay out enclosures and build bridges between or over them.

Again! Again!

The schema can further be seen in children's actions and play when they become fascinated with building things such as fences, prisons and barricades, and practitioners can respond by offering daily access to construction and creative materials, unit and hollow blocks, blankets, junk modelling and other resources for creating and constructing imaginative enclosures.

The enclosure schema enables children to order, combine, place and bridge things to form enclosed spaces. They may also be exploring how things will get in and out of their enclosures. Some children make enclosures for farm animals but leave an opening so the animals can get in and out, or build big enclosures with smaller ones inside. Children who are interested in enclosures may also arrange objects or food around the edge of a plate or run or ride bikes round and round in an enclosed space.

Practitioners should recognise that children exploring the enclosure schema will select individual experiences that suit their own interests. For example:

> Four boys, aged four, are playing with blocks, making tall and long enclosures. Their construction is not only symmetrical but it has many layers built upwards. The boys tell the practitioner they are building a multi-storey zoo.

> Joy, aged four has a fascination for birds in cages. Her childminder notices that Joy often draws detailed pictures of these and birds and ducks on ponds, carefully enclosing them with lines.

> Alex, a three-year-old boy in nursery class gathers cushions, and is unwilling to share them with other children. He carefully places the cushions around himself to form an enclosure when sitting on the carpet.

These examples of the enclosing schemas gives us valuable insight into how schematic actions might at first appear to be confusing or annoying, but observation and sensitive discussion with the children will clarify what is happening, and when a child is absorbed in repeated or schema play.

Just as areas of learning interlink, so do different schemas, and the enclosing schema has strong links with the trajectory, enveloping and rotation schemas.

The enveloping schema

The enveloping schema is often seen when children cover objects or themselves with all sorts of materials, and this schema can often be observed at the same time as a child is exploring the enclosure schema.

Children with the enveloping schema are interested in covering over, camouflaging, hiding and concealing themselves and objects. They may be observed dressing up in hats, scarves, with necklaces, bracelets, bangles, earrings, nail varnish and rings. They make dens, hide under blankets, behind furniture or in cupboards; they may turn themselves into a ghost by wearing a sheet; they fill bags with bits and pieces; they paint or glue all over their hands and then peel it off, or paint all over a picture with a single colour.

> Hannah, aged four is playing with cardboard tubes, she is interested in the way some tubes fit inside each other, some disappearing completely. She plays for some time this way before making the tubes into a telescope and playing I-Spy.

As with all lines of enquiry, children begin to make connections in their learning by finding answers to their questions using everyday interactions with people and the environment. When they are satisfied with their findings they may simply move on to a new line of exploration, which may have the same underlying pattern, and the schema becomes more and more sophisticated. Chris Athey suggests that children pay attention to materials and experiences around them, which in turn feed their schema.

Practitioners should be aware of the sorts of questions children are asking themselves as they play, as well as the sorts of questions practitioners might pose to the children, and it may be helpful to try to think like children, when deciding what children might need. This co-thinking ensures that practitioners provide children with inspiring resources - somewhere to hide, materials for wrapping and building dens, different types of sticky tape and other fixing materials, dressing up clothes, hats, shoes, handbags and containers along with objects for filling and containment.

The transporting schema

The transporting schema can be recognised when children become intent on moving objects or themselves from place to place, carrying objects in their hands or pockets or filling bags, buckets and containers and then transporting these to be scattered or piled up at different locations. They will often push empty or full buggies, carts, prams and wheelbarrows around, or use trolleys, bikes, bags and rucksacks to move a variety of objects. This interest in transporting may be based on their own first hand experiences of being transported in vehicles, buggies, or the arms of adults.

> **Charlotte and Austin, both aged three, are playing with buggies. Charlotte has a doll in her buggy and is trying to persuade Austin to do the same. Austin moves away from Charlotte, refusing to put a doll in his buggy. When Charlotte forcibly puts a doll in Austin's buggy, Austin throws it out, shouting, 'No, no dolly!'.**

This observation is an example of schematic behaviour following a logical path. Austin is still exploring the idea of travelling from place to place and the presence of the doll in a buggy is not his current interest. The experience of moving himself and the buggy around the setting is sufficient for Austin, where Charlotte has made a connection between putting a doll in her buggy and moving it from place to place. Over time and with more experience, Austin's play may develop into putting objects in a buggy or other wheeled container and moving with them from one place to another.

Practitioners can value children's needs to move objects from one place to another by observing children's interests and providing appropriate resources for play. Behaviour that could be referred to as flitting, merely moving from activity to activity without properly participating in any one, may now be seen as purposeful, and children will benefit from practitioners who can support their desire to carry and remove objects by providing them with opportunities to do so both indoors and outside.

How practitioners respond to children moving equipment is crucial, and they may need to be flexible and understanding when sand and water are mixed together, or playdough is transported from the messy play table to be used in the home corner. One benefit may be that children demonstrating the transporting schema often enjoy tidying up time and putting things away!

The connecting schema

Children involved in the connecting schema often show a fascination with joining things together, fastening or tying things using rope, string, tape, staples or glue. They may be connecting pieces of wood with nails and glue, linking and joining recycled materials at a craft table, or fastening fabrics and scarves in role play. They may join wheeled toys in the garden or suspend objects from fences, bushes or themselves, often linking objects in very complex ways.

As the connecting schema evolves, disconnection sometimes becomes as important as connection, untying as important as tying and, as children begin to explore the idea of separating things, they often demolish items they have previously constructed, or take toys apart. They may take the wheels off toy cars, disconnect all the pieces in a construction set, untie knots, bows or fastenings.

Josh, aged four, collects up all the trains and track at his nursery. He is adamant that he is not going to let the other children connect the track and run the trains. This is unusual behaviour for him, as he is usually helpful and willing to join the rest of the group, helping other children to do up their buttons or zips and tie their laces (another form of connection).

Four boys are observed playing with a large box, which they are making into a pizza shop, using the flaps on both sides of the box as doors. They decide they would like to make pizza deliveries, and they need to fasten the doors back to stop them from swinging closed. One of the boys spends some time absorbed in making this work by using string and elastic, continuing even after the rest of the group have abandoned the pizza play.

Again! Again!

Between the ages of four and five, children using the connecting schema should have frequent and free access to building, woodwork and creative materials, with a wide variety of different sorts of joining materials. Practitioners should also consider how they offer construction toys and other toys with connections, understanding the need for disconnection as well as connection. Observing children in their free and unrestricted play will give practitioners valuable insight into the way children are using this schema to make sense of the world.

The positioning schema

A pattern of play that involves children in positioning, ordering and arranging objects or their own bodies is referred to as a positioning schema. Some children may become obsessed with the exact placing of objects or their own bodies - on top of, underneath, in front of, around the edge of, behind or next to a particular toy, person or object. As with other schemas, positioning may also contain elements of the trajectory and connecting schemas, as young children line up toys and other objects in rows and sort them into groups, lining up cars, dolls, animals, books, in order of size and shape. The positioning schema may also be seen as children place objects carefully in rows, form queues and insist on this order in other children. The may also arrange paper or books in tidy piles, or create patterns in rows and lines in mark marking and construction play.

Hector, aged four, is sorting transport vehicles and placing them in groups. He parks three rows of cars, organising them by colour, lines up the trains in a long line, flies his aeroplanes high and brings them down to land in a careful line.

Children with this schema may sometimes demonstrate unusual behaviour, such as not wanting different foods mixed together on the same plate, or lining up their toys or other objects in order of shape and size in unconventional places, such as by the front door. This behaviour is often incorrectly regarded by practitioners or parents as having elements of an 'Obsessive Compulsive Disorder' (OCD), and practitioners may need to reassure parents and colleagues that the positioning schema, like all schemas, is part of learning, and is how children make sense of their experiences, testing their knowledge again and again as they confirm and organise what they know and understand, extending their growing ability to think logically and apply order in and through their play.

The orientation schema

Babies are born to move. When they lie on their tummies or backs they see their world from a particular viewpoint, but things start to look different for them as they learn to roll, sit up, crawl, stand and climb, discovering the effect of movement and the difference they can make to their view of the world. The orientation schema is linked to the positioning and rotation schemas, as children experiment with seeing things from different viewpoints, and two or three schemas are often explored at the same time.

The orientation schema may be observed in children's actions when they start to look at the world from different angles. They may hang upside down, look through their legs, turn objects upside down to view them, do head over heels, cartwheels and handstands, and enjoy rocking on the rocking horse or climbing trees and ladders to get a new view on life. Other features of orienting behaviour may include building and using ramps, rocking on chairs, climbing hills and slopes, sliding down banisters, rolling, climbing and standing on ledges and objects to get a higher position. A pattern may emerge in children's actions that links orientation with angles, slopes and shapes as children explore how different objects and their own bodies move on various surfaces.

> **Lars, aged five, is in the garden area of his nursery class moving around on all fours. He is pretending to be a spider, which involves climbing, scurrying, and moving forwards sideways and backwards. Later, he is observed playing with a toy tractor, repeatedly driving it forwards, backwards, through spaces and round corners.**

Children exploring the orientation schema may have a problem sitting still and may fidget during group times, needing a physical object such as a finger puppet, some playdough or a beanbag to help them concentrate. Practitioners also need to offer plenty of play opportunities to support individuals in developing and coordinating their physical movements as they explore current interests in freely chosen play.

Schemas, although they can be categorised and named in the way outlined here, do not always appear so clearly in every child. Some children never seem to demonstrate a clear schematic behaviour that can be named, others may spend days or weeks in concentrated play exploring through clearly observed activities which can be noted, supported and extended by practitioners. Other children combine several schemas at the same time, moving smoothly from one to another.

What is vital is that we recognise the importance of children's self-initiated play and the role of the sensitive adult in providing the time, place and opportunity to turn purposeful play into learning.

Again! Again!

Supporting children's schema play

In this chapter you will find some longer observations of babies and children in action, exploring the major schemas as they play. These are amplified by comments on what the individual observations might be telling us about children's learning and development, and ideas for activities and resources that could be offered in support of a current schema.

We are <u>not</u> suggesting that children's play and learning should be channelled, but that practitioners should be aware of the way in which familiar resources and equipment can be made available to support individuals and groups involved in particular schemas. A rich and varied environment, and freedom to explore it, will support children as they play. It is the responsibility of the practitioner to ensure that schematic play is noticed, valued and given time.

The following schemas are explored:

Trajectory
Orientation
Connecting
Rotation
Enclosing
Enveloping
Positioning
Transporting

Trajectory schemas in action

Definition: An interest in how objects and people move, and how children can affect that movement. This schema can be seen in children's actions when they drop objects, jump, swing and climb up and down repeatedly.

What happens?

Joseph, aged nine months, and Sky, aged ten months, are at nursery playing a game with the practitioner. The practitioner places a cap on Sky's head. Sky removes the cap by swiping her head with her hands. The cap falls at her side. The practitioner mimicks Sky's facial response and repeats the action, telling the babies that the cap is falling down. Sky picks up the cap and spends some time examining it, passing it from hand to hand.

The practitioner then covers her eyes with some mesh. The babies respond excitedly. The practitioner places the mesh on Joseph's head and watches him as he tracks her hand with his eyes. Joseph looks up for the mesh then down, at first he does not realise that the practitioner has left the mesh on his head. He becomes excited and rocks his body back and forth. The practitioner tells the babies, 'It's falling down'. Joseph examines the mesh, poking his fingers through the weave. After a few moments play, Joseph shows his delight by kicking his legs and waving his arms as he waits in anticipation for the mesh to fall down again.

What does this observation tell us?

'Two early schemas are tracking objects and gazing at objects. Gazing leads to knowledge of configuration. Tracking leads to knowledge of movement aspects of object, including self and other persons.'   *Chris Athey*

At birth, tracking and gazing are two separate behaviours. Joseph's behaviour illustrates that he knows that an object or person can be still or that they can

Again! Again!   —

move. His tracking and gazing are no longer separate, and he can track a moving object. His early interactions and experiences have enabled him to co-ordinate these very early sensori-motor schemas.

The practitioner did this activity with Joseph after observing him dropping objects from his cot. Joseph is showing some knowledge of movement, space and cause and effect.

A pattern of trajectory actions can be seen in Joseph's movements as he tracks the falling cap. Joseph is displaying an interest in vertical movements, and his exploration involves tracking and trial and error. He solved the problem of the mesh on his head through his back and forth sensori-motor movements. He showed his enjoyment of the experience by rocking. The more the game was repeated the more he enjoyed it.

'From six months, when toys fall from the infant's hand, he or she will watch the fall to the point of arrival, providing all the action is within the visual field.'
Mary Sheridan

What do other babies and children do?

Babies will hold and inspect objects by staring at them. They will mouth, shake, drop, throw and bang objects. They will explore vertical and horizontal movements by placing one thing on top of, or next to another, lining up toys, opening and closing drawers, going in and out of doors, running up and down stairs, steps or corridors, turning switches off and on and when pushed forward and back in a buggy.

Toddlers may explore distances by dropping toys, and they may begin to make vertical and horizontal structures in their drawings and construction. Children may then move on to coordinating horizontal and vertical lines into crosses and grids.

'Provide materials that support particular schemas, for example, things to throw for a child who is exploring trajectory.'
EYFS

'Imagination is more important than knowledge. To raise questions, new possibilities, to regard an old problem from a new angle requires creative imagination and makes a real advance in science.'
Albert Einstein

Again! Again!

The trajectory schema

Definition: An interest in how objects and people move, and how children can affect that movement. This schema can be seen in children's actions when they drop objects, jump, swing and climb up and down repeatedly.

Some resources and activities

For exploring

- Blow feathers, tissue paper or chiffon scarves.
- Make simple folded paper planes and see how they fly.
- Make a simple pulley system. Try www.mindstretchers.co.uk for a simple pulley system.
- Play dropping different objects on to a target. Choose objects of different weights and shapes.

Creative play

- Fill clean spray bottles and squeezy bottles with thin paint. Spray paint on to different colours and textures of paper.
- Fold and decorate simple paper planes to throw.
- Tie a length of string on to big paint brushes and paint with a pendulum action.
- Line a tray with paper and dip marbles in paint and roll over the paper.
- Make simple kites, flags and bunting.

Messy play

- Chase and catch bubbles. Google 'Make bubbles' for bubble making ideas and bubble mixture recipes.
- Use pipes and funnels in a water tray to explore how water moves.
- Splat wet sponges at a target.
- Dribble runny paint from a brush or dropper on to a vertical mirror or paper clipped to an easel.
- Use a water pump, funnels and plastic piping to make moving water.
- Dribble coloured water from droppers or fingers down mirrors.

For inspiration

- Google Images - space, kites, flying
- Kites, pin wheels, flags and bunting.
- Pulleys and pendulums.

The treasure basket

- Chiffon or silky scarves to blow.
- Feathers, sycamore keys and leaves to drop.
- Lengths of fabric to twirl, flick, spin.
- Different sizes and weights of balls for throwing, spinning and rolling.

Fine motor

- Try some simple yo-yos.
- Spin, twirl, throw hoops or quoits.
- Post cars or small balls down different lengths of tubing.
- Run with kites and streamers.
- Explore objects that bounce.
- Flick small balls of paper with a flexible ruler at a target.
- Attach lengths of elastic to very light ping-pong balls with holes and experiment.
- Build helicopters and small planes with plastic interconnecting blocks.
- Build with straws and sticky tape objects that are light enough to fly or spin when thrown.

Outside

- Provide soft and harder balls of different sizes, weights and textures to bounce, roll and throw.
- Allow children to swing and jump safely.
- Bounce on a mini trampoline.
- Fill plastic water bottles and use a small ball for simple skittle play.
- Use soft toys and hoops to create a 'Hoopla'.
- Try plastic croquet or a plastic golf set.
- Bat lots of different sized balls or balloons up and down.
- Make tracks and slalom courses for bikes and other wheeled toys.

Stories, rhymes & songs

- Read _The Lighthouse Keeper's Lunch_, and talk about pulleys.
- Check out how balloons fly through the air and share _Balloon_ by Jez Alborough, or _The Blue Balloon_ by Mick Inkpen.
- For some flying tales, try _Some Dogs Do_ by Jez Alborough, or _Pigs Can't Fly_ by Ben Cort.
- Play with bouncy things to: _What Bounces?_ by Kate Duke, _Bounce_ by Doreen Cronin, or _Emily Loves to Bounce_ by Stephen King.

Equipment to buy/find

- _Usborne Book of Kites_ by Susie Mays and Angie Sage.
- Kites, flags and bunting.
- Spinners and simple airplanes.
- Google 'Easy paper plane templates'.

Key words

- fly, spin, twirl
- glide, float, drop
- bounce high low
- heavy light
- land, target, take off
- swing, pendulum, pulley
- up, down, fast, slow, high, low

Supporting schema play

Rotation schemas in action

Definition: An interest in things which turn, such as knobs, taps, keys, wind-up toys. This schema can also be seen in children's actions when they run or ride bikes round in circles or spin round and round, or make circle and spiral patterns in paint or other messy play.

What happens?

When Jade, aged three years, arrives at the home of her childminder she is observed making slow circular movements holding a torn transparent fruit bag. Later she starts drawing circles. She draws a large circle, the size of a saucer on her paper. Inside the large circle she draws five smaller circles reducing in size to that of a penny. As she draws, she makes corresponding circular movements with her other hand. During play she is also seen twisting, turning and occasionally flicking her hair in circles, while looking at a book and while holding a doll.

The childminder also notices Jade pushing her doll in its buggy round in circles and saying. 'We going round and round,' at the same time making circular movements with her arms.

What does this observation tell us?

Jade is exploring her surrounding space in movement by going round and round. She is sensing rotation through her own movement and actions, enabling her to develop a better understanding of the mechanics of rotation. A pattern of this schema runs through Jade's actions and can be seen when she turns her whole body and the buggy round and her mark making as she uses enclosed lines in her drawing.

The rotation schema has a powerful impact on children's sensori-motor movements and actions. It may be observed running through all their active learning and play. In Jade's case, it can be seen to be building on what she already knows about rotation.

_____ **Again! Again!** _____

'The caregiver might introduce a variety of interesting rotational experiences, from spinning tops to washing machines, and the nursery rhymes which are about rotating, like Ring o' Roses.' John Matthews

'Emotionally and intellectually rich childhoods that allow involvement and play in natural biological schemas quite literally lead to richer brains.' Seymour Papert

What do other babies and children do?

The sensori-motor rotational schema is frequently seen in the play of babies and young children. Babies may be observed sitting up, using their bottom, legs and feet to swivel and rotate themselves around again and again, exploring and discovering how to move in a circular direction using objects and themselves. Some children may go round and round a column or pole, or run round in circles until they are dizzy. Pulling toys round and round on a string, making circular scribbles in their drawing and paintings, rolling up paper or their own drawings and paintings may also be a feature of play. Four-year-olds are often observed functioning at a high level when they construct and build objects with rotating parts or explore curved lines and going round a boundary in their mark making and drawing.

'To be effective, the curriculum content offered to children must find a match in the content of their thinking and with their capabilities.' Cathy Nutbrown

Asking children about their rotational movements and actions when they are happening, and talking to them will help practitioners tune into the sensations babies and young children are exploring.

'There is a need for adults to extend learning through appropriate language in genuine conversations. Genuine conversation seems to arise more often when adults have an understanding of schemas and so tune into what the child says.' Marion Whitehead

Supporting schema play

Again! Again!

The rotation schema

Definition: An interest in things which turn, such as knobs, taps, keys, wind-up toys. This schema can also be seen in children's actions when they run or ride bikes round in circles or spin round and round, or make circle and spiral patterns in paint or other messy play.

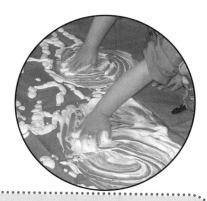

Some resources and activities

For exploring

- Locks and keys.
- Wind-up toys.
- 'Cogs' construction toy.
- Musical boxes and music toys.
- Bring a bike in so the children can explore big wheels.
- Analogue clocks and watches with hands and winders.
- Spirals - snail shells, coils, springs.
- Kaleidoscopes of all sorts.
- Football rattles, tops, globes.
- Food mixers and liquidisers.

Creative Play

- Mixing and stirring.
- Ribbons and ribbon sticks.
- CD players or an old record player.
- Hang CDs from coat hangers or string for mobiles.
- Make your own simple windmills and spiral windsocks.
- Bake Swiss roll or cheese whizzers (spiral cheese cookies) or make spiral sandwiches.
- Make simple kaleidoscopes.
- Put water wheels in the water tray or guttering.

Messy play

- Let the children mix their own dough using a simple recipe.
- Offer dry and cooked pasta for mixing and stirring.
- Get a salad spinner to use with paint or painty marbles.
- Make bubbly water with rotary whisks.
- Roll painty balls down slopes or in a paddling pool.
- Spin painty chains on big sheets of paper on the floor.
- Use paint rollers of all sorts..

For inspiration

- Big wheel, London Eye.
- Roundabouts of all sorts.
- Helicopters, propellers.
- Helter skelter and other rides.
- Maypole dancing.

The treasure basket

- Bowls and all sorts of spoons.
- Spinners.
- Bracelets and bangles.
- Rolling and spinning rattles.
- Spiral bead rattles.
- Cotton reels.

Again! Again!

Fine motor

- Use icing pens and tubes to make spiral patterns on biscuits.
- Roll balls into boxes and baskets.
- Offer spanners and screwdrivers.
- Provide screw toys.
- Construction toys with wheels - Mobilo, Lego, Constructo-straws etc.
- Pencil sharpeners.
- Hand operated sewing machine.
- Make ramps and runways for big and little wheels; and old CDs, round container lids, aerosol tops, or reels.
- Cogs and cog sets.

Outside

- Provide lots of soft and harder balls of different sizes and shapes.
- Roll CDs down slides and slopes.
- Paint or chalk circles and spirals on the ground for riding, running, rolling, jumping, spinning.
- Suspend a rope or tyre from a climbing frame or tree, so children can hang and spin.
- Hoop-la or quoits.
- Simple roundabouts.
- Woodwork with screwdrivers and hand held drills.
- Ribbon sticks, windmills.
- Hang spinning things, or objects on strings from bushes and trees.
- Watch sycamore seeds (helicopters) falling from the trees.

Stories, rhymes & songs

All ring games give the 'round and round' sensation and can be sung and played indoors and outside. Some examples are:
- Here we go Round the Mulberry Bush.
- Round and Round the Village.
- The Wheels on the Bus.
- Round and Round the Garden.

Some stories:
- One Round Moon and a Star for Me; The Wheels on the Bus; Round Like a Ball; The Village of Round and Square Houses

Equipment to buy/find

- Light spinners (from www.spacekraft.co.uk)
- Fishing rod reels, rolls of string, twine, wool, rope.
- Hand operated sewing machine.
- Locks, fans
- Wheels of all sorts

Key words

- fly
- spin
- twirl
- round
- circle
- twist
- faster and faster
- dizzy
- spiral
- helicopter

Enclosing schemas in action

Definition: An interest in creating and/or occupying enclosed spaces. It can be seen in children's actions as they create structures in which they sometimes enclose themselves or objects. Some spaces may be left empty, others may be filled with objects.

What happens?

The practitioner observes Ben and Oliver building a large block enclosure using long wooden planks. They use shorter planks to close in the gaps they are creating. Inside the enclosure, they build three vertical hollow structures. Ben places two blocks between the hollow structures to act as spacers. They then place smaller blocks inside the larger hollow blocks. The boys stand back to look at the structure. Oliver puts another hollow block on one of the vertical structures. Ben tells him that they only have one of the big blocks left. Oliver removes the block, saying it makes it too high. The boys add cars, placing and parking them inside another enclosed area, and make an enclosed garden, using cylinders to represent plants, flowers and trees.

What does this observation tell us?

'In play a child always behaves beyond his average age, above his daily behaviour; in play it is as though he were a head taller than himself.'

Lev Vygotsky

Ben and Oliver are exploring straight lines and angles. When they explained what they had made, they said the enclosure represented the estate they live in, three blocks of flats and the environment surrounding them. Ben shows his understanding of space and measurement by placing the two blocks between hollow blocks as spacers, to ensure that they were of equal distance apart.

Schematic play experiences help children to represent their thoughts, feelings and ideas symbolically. Oliver shows knowledge about and an understanding of height. Ben shows knowledge and understanding of space, separations and proximity. The boys work together talking about where they are going to place the car park and garden, showing an understanding of planning and mapping. Ben's and Oliver's schemas can be seen to be following a particular path that involves

Again! Again!

creating and filling in a series of different enclosures.

'Young children need to have powerful experiences through which to, 'select' items, for representation. They need opportunities to use their 'roles' to 'generalise' behaviours, and to translate between modes.'   Tina Bruce

What do other babies and children do?

Young children are sometimes observed building 'Bridging Enclosures' as they begin to make connections between different structures and enclosures. They may make other enclosures with straight and angled lines. Most children who build enclosures fill them in an ordered way. The enclosure schema has close ties with trajectory, connecting, enveloping and positioning schemas and practitioners may often observe enclosure behaviour combined with other schemas.

'When children reach the 'thought level' the earlier motor and representational stages, with all the contents of past experience, are 'brought forward' to provide the 'form' and 'stuff' of thinking.'   Chris Athey

The enclosing schema

Definition: An interest in creating and/or occupying enclosed spaces. It can be seen in children's actions as they create structures in which they sometimes enclose themselves or objects. Some spaces may be left empty, others may be filled with objects.

Some resources and activities

For exploring

- Provide a quiet corner where children can build an oasis for reflection or simply watching the activities.
- Drape a sheet over a frame to create a small den or hidey hole for one or two children at a time. Offer floor cushions, blankets, a few soft toys and some books.
- Help the children to add a semi-transparent door from net or lace.

Creative play

- Make bracelets and bangles.
- Cut watches or jewellery from catalogues, stick to thin card and tape around the child's wrist.
- Make borders and picture frames.
- Draw around other children.
- Sit in the centre of a hoop and create pictures and patterns on the floor in chalk or paint around the edge.
- Make cloaks, hats, masks.
- Zoo and farm small world play, play people, houses, fences, bricks for wall.

Messy play

- Use lolly sticks and twigs to build fences, roads and bridges in sand.
- Roll dough to make enclosures.
- Transform shoe boxes into houses or beds for small world figures.
- Wrap plaster bandages around hands or feet to create sculptures.
- Use natural materials to weave and build nests.
- Create burrows and tunnels in very wet sand.
- Use clay to make caves.

Make tents & shelters

- Blankets and netting.
- Large cardboard boxes.
- Pop-up tents, gazebos, sheds.
- Tunnels, hollow cubes, cupboards.

The treasure basket

- Rings, bracelets, watches, bangles and necklaces.
- Hats and gloves, saris, stoles.
- Scarves, lengths of ribbon, braid and tinsel.
- Bandages, arm and knee supports

Again! Again!

Construction

- Make fences, walls, and enclosures for miniature animals and play people.
- Buy some huge rolls of cardboard packaging material.
- Build walls, edges, borders, arcs, curves and bridges.
- Build dens.
- Experiment with the construction of willow dens and other structures.
- Construct screens from netting or semi-transparent material.
- Create dens with doors from large cardboard boxes.
- Use the tool bench and woodwork tools to create enclosures.

Outside

- Offer tape and lengths of ribbon to enclose spaces, block entrances, make shelters.
- With chalk, mark out spaces and places.
- Drape fabric over frames or a washing line, secure with pegs or bulldog clips.
- Create a dome for parachute games.
- Add paper or fabric doors to barrels and tunnels.
- Use large cardboard boxes as garages and sheds for bicycles and as hidey holes.
- Use boxes, cartons and other recycled materials to make houses and homes for small world characters.

Stories, rhymes & songs

- Traditional stories such as _The Three Little Pigs_.
- Thomas the Tank Engine stories about tunnels and bridges.
- _Lark in the Ark_ by Peter Bently and Lynne Chapman.
- _Ten in the Bed_ - a counting down rhyme with lots of opportunities for simple pretend play.
- _Little Roo and the Big Wide World_ by Guido van Genechelen.
- _My Cat Likes to Hide in Boxes_ by Eve Sutton and Lynley Dodd.

Equipment to buy/find

- Living willow, twigs, canes, raffia, mosses, card and paper rolls.
- Different types of string, pegs and fasteners and tape.
- Blankets, curtains and throws.
- Saris and lengths of fabric/plastic.
- Large cardboard boxes.

Key words

- position and size words
- enclose, wrap, contain
- safe
- inside, outside
- boundary, edge, margin
- corner, side
- entrance, exit,
- way in, way out

Enveloping schemas in action

Definition: An interest in covering and wrapping up objects or themselves or in putting things inside bags, baskets and containers. Sometimes children will drape themselves in fabrics or clothing such as hoods, hats, gloves, cloaks, or become interested in wrapping things and securing them with string or tape.

What happens?

A practitioner is observing Annabelle, aged three, putting on layers of dressing up clothes. Later Annabelle is observed wrapping large and small boxes and securing them with masking tape. She layers a piece of paper with masking tape until it is completely covered. The practitioner observes Annabelle covering another piece of paper using brown packing tape. She covers the paper, back and front. She then covers a smaller piece of paper. She folds the large paper in half. She folds over some tape to make it sticky on both sides and uses it to stick the papers together. She then puts it all inside one of her wrapped boxes.

What does this observation tell us?

'A child's way, often their favourite way, of exploring the world at a given time. Schemas include a combination of activities and ideas that shape a child's current approach to learning.'   *Jennie Lindon*

Annabelle is using the enveloping schema throughout this observation. It can be seen in her actions as she envelopes herself with layers of dressing-up clothes and when she does exactly the same with the boxes and paper, using masking and packing tape. Annabelle is exploring the idea of hiding, dressing-up and concealing.

She is exploring two related lines of enquiry, covering over objects and covering up herself. Annabelle uses different materials to aid her in covering the whole surface of her paper. She used her own version of double-sided tape to ensure that her smaller paper stayed in place.

'Children's schemas can be viewed as part of their motivation for learning, their insatiable drive to move, represent, discuss, question and find out.'
Cathy Nutbrown

Again! Again!   —

What do other babies and children do?

Some children may put things into bags or purses, wrap themselves in blankets, like being cuddled, cover over paintings with a single colour or scribble over drawings. Although they can no longer see the picture, they know that it is underneath the paint. Other children will use a range of materials to wrap, cover, layer, wrap up themselves or furniture with stickytape and masking tape, or fill models and constructions with small objects. Children also demonstrate the enveloping schema by trying on and wearing a succession of shoes and boots or gloves. They fill boxes or bags with objects or post objects through gaps, holes and spaces. They also take pleasure in hiding objects and themselves.

'They can get into spaces where they can hide.'
Chris Athey

The enveloping schema

Definition: An interest in covering and wrapping up objects or themselves or in putting things inside bags, baskets and containers. Sometimes children drape themselves in fabrics or clothing such as hoods, hats, gloves, cloaks, or wrap and secure things with string or tape.

Some resources and activities

Construction

- Build giant 'Pass the Parcel' bundles, wrap pretend gifts, fill crates with plastic bottles.
- Fill large tubes with sheets of paper or bits of fabric to push, pull, wrap and stuff.
- Experiment with paper, card, hole punch, treasure tags, twisty tags, cable ties and sticky tape.
- Really long lengths of fabric to twist, turn, wrap and roll in.

Creative play

- Stuff old socks to make snakes.
- Make sock and glove puppets.
- Make your own feely bags/boxes.
- Make 'lift the flap' books/pictures.
- Offer simple templates to create masks, hats and crowns.
- Supply lots of mark makers, envelopes, boxes, gift bags.
- Experiment with layering coloured cellophane and tracing paper with some very thin paint mixed with a little PVA glue or paste.
- Wearing gloves make hand prints.
- Wrap pictures in clear sticky tape.
- Layer collage materials.

Messy play

- Make pasta parcels or wraps.
- Offer different shapes, thicknesses and types of paper for folding.
- Fill containers with sand, water, jelly, gloop, dough, cooked pasta.
- Zip-lock or paper bags to fill with dry pasta, beans, sequins, sand.
- Use rollers and big brushes to paint layers of paint on big boxes.
- Make tiny fruit jellies or fruit cubes in ice-cube trays.
- Cover balloons with string and lengths of coloured and shiny paper, soaked in wallpaper paste.

For inspiration

- Ships in bottles.
- Treasure boxes with keys.
- Origami and folded paper fans.

The treasure basket

- Fabric for wrapping and covering - fleece, cotton, fur fabric, suede, satin, wool, plastic, bubble wrap, net curtain, silky scarves.
- Nesting boxes, card tubes, glasses cases, purses, wallets, jewel boxes.

Again! Again!

Fine motor

- Nesting toys and Russian dolls.
- Billie's barrels.
- Shape-sorting toys, posting toys.
- Folding, tearing, cutting, sticking, wrapping pretend gifts.
- Toys with doors and keys.
- Paint programs on the computer to create layers.
- Try Kim's memory game.
- Jack-in-the-box and other surprise or pop-up toys.
- Prepare and then wrap up tiny bits of fruit in twists of cellophane for snack time.
- Purses, boxes, little tins and gift boxes or bags to fill.

Stories, rhymes & songs

- Build a House with Five Bricks.
- Tommy Thumb.
- Five Fat Peas in a Pea Pod Pressed.
- Here is the Beehive.
- Five Eggs and Five Eggs.
- Miss Polly had a Dolly.
- Read Kipper's Toybox by Mick Inkpen or The Shopping Basket by John Burningham.
- Wrap dolls or soft toys in blankets and sing Ten in the Bed.
- Here is a Box and Here is a Lid.

Outside

- Building and playing in dens and shelters.
- Parachute play.
- Small blankets, dolls, soft toys and pushchairs.
- Big and small boxes/containers.
- Bags, baskets, buckets, suitcases and boxes for collections of objects.
- Bark area for digging and burying.
- Suitcases of dressing-up clothes.
- Capes, net curtains, saris.
- Wrap outside toys with newspapers and tape.
- Block and tackle pulley system for filling and emptying.
- Bandages, headphones, gloves, hats and scarves.
- Dolls' blankets and sheets.

Equipment to buy/find

- Net curtains, survival blankets, camouflage fabric or netting.
- Russian dolls, nesting toys.
- Lengths of fabric.
- Parachute, tents.
- Transparent paper and cellophane.

Key words

- under, over, in and on
- above and below
- size words
- visible, invisible
- transparent/opaque
- here/gone
- hidden
- wrap/unwrap
- full /empty

Transporting schemas in action

Definition: An interest in moving themselves around and in transporting objects. Once they are mobile, babies and children begin to move objects and themselves from one place to another, using bags, bikes, trucks etc.

What happens?

CJ chooses a wooden truck and wants to transport children around the garden. He likes stopping frequently to let children get on and off. He tells the practitioner that he was playing 'I'm a bus driver'. Later, he plays a game where he is a delivery driver. He transports buckets of water and a bag on the back of his truck. He drives his truck around all the obstacles in the garden, and stops at the sandpit to give the buckets of water to the children playing there. He gets back on his truck and rides it to the other end of the garden to find his friend Angela, and returns her bag which she had mislaid earlier.

What does this observation tell us?

CJ is selective about what he transports, matching the objects being transported with the particular roles of being a bus driver then later a delivery driver. CJ's play had real purpose and commonalities that relate to carrying people and objects around. CJ is clearly motivated by the idea of collecting and transporting people and objects. CJ was exploring distance, making journeys, and speed as he moved children and water to different end points around the garden. CJ's interest in playing transporting games can be seen to be following a particular path in that all his actions in his play are about journeys and transporting.

'The intensity with which children use a currently compelling schema can not be mistaken.'   *Mollie Davis*

What do other babies and children do?

Toddlers may be observed transporting their cups or comfort objects and giving them to people. They may want to put things in and take them out of bags or containers to transport them. Other children may show an interest in anything that can be pushed - buggies, cars and wheelbarrows - or things that they can carry objects in, such as baskets, rucksacks, bags, toy cranes and shopping trolleys.

Again! Again!

Older children may develop an interest in games such as postmen or delivery drivers, having picnics or attaching brooms to trucks to sweep up the leaves and transport them. Children can be observed taking teddies and dolls out in buggies, prams and car seats or transporting planks, crates, and bricks around. One unfortunately irritating aspect of this schema is that children may remove equipment from inside to use in their play outside or conversely bring in sand to put into the home corner.

> '*Objects look different when scattered about or heaped together. But they are of the same quantity even though their appearance changes. The transporting schema leads towards a concept of quantity.*'   Tina Bruce

The transporting schema

Definition: An interest in moving themselves around and in transporting objects. Once they are mobile, babies and children begin to move objects and themselves from one place to another, using bags, bikes, trucks etc.

Some resources and activities

Sand and water play

- Add gravel, shells and pebbles to diggers, dumpers and tractors in wet or dry sand.
- Transport small bricks and stones in barges and boats in water play.
- Use scoops and spades to fill and empty sand moulds in wet sand.
- Build waterways with guttering and sail twigs and sticks.
- Use plastic jugs and bottles to move water about outside.

Boxes and baskets

- Provide purses, shopping baskets and trolleys, small suitcases, hand-bags, rucksacks, drawstring bags.
- Provide sets of stacking boxes and containers, graded by size for filling with different objects.
- Play a circle time game where each child shows items from a collection in a bag or basket.
- Use strings of necklaces and beads to fill and empty pretty bags.

Outside

- Use wheelbarrows, carts and trolleys with different size boxes.
- Chalk paths, roadways or even a small maze on the ground.
- Provide buckets and bags for collecting natural objects.
- Fill old milk crates with plastic water bottles. Create a milk round.
- Collect seeds, grasses, leaves and petals in brown paper bags.
- Provide bricks, logs, cobbles, rockery stones, bags of compost for children to carry round in barrows.
- Offer pulleys, ropes and wire for transporting buckets and boxes.

Specially for babies

- Fill a shiny tin with interesting objects to pull out and replace.
- Gather together small, easily opened bags and baskets and fill with small soft toys or objects.
- Provide tiny shopping baskets and bags for collecting.
- Fill a purse with brightly coloured safe lengths of string and ribbon.
- Offer toys that roll and move easily.
- Create a treasure basket of everyday objects for filling and emptying as well as exploring.
- Offer an empty washing up bowl with plastic cups, spoons, plates.

Again! Again!

More filling & emptying

- Use tiny spoons and scoops to fill and empty ice cube trays with flour, rice or pulses.
- Fill and empty huge boxes with cushions and bean bags.
- Stuff lengths of fabric into pillow-cases and enjoy emptying again.
- Fill and empty egg cups, cake cases and other small containers with buttons and sequins.
- Use plastic droppers and colouring for different filling and emptying play.
- Fill old envelopes with pictures torn from catalogues and magazines.
- Chalk tracks and roadways on table tops or the floor as paths for transported goods to travel along.

Imaginative play

- Provide lots of opportunities for babies and young children to empty and fill baskets of clothes, cupboards full of pots and pans and so on, in the home corner.
- Use some cold tea for some real tea-set play.
- Make a pretend washing machine and fill and empty it with clothes.
- Fill and empty an old satchel or shoulder bag with envelopes for some postal deliveries.
- Read picture story books about moving house, and provide big cardboard boxes for the children to pack up and move soft toys and other light objects.

Stories, rhymes & songs

- _Teddy Bears' Moving Day_ by Susanna Getz.
- _The Shopping Basket_ by John Burningham.
- _Push Pull, Empty, Full_ by Tana Hoban.
- _Jack in a Box_ by Julia Jarman.
- _Big Red Bath_ by Julia Jarman.
- _Diggers and Dumpers_, and _Tough Machines_ by DK.
- _Duck in a Truck_ by Martin Waddell.

Equipment to buy/find

- Bags, baskets, and boxes.
- Graded stacking boxes.
- Scoops, spoons, small containers.
- Big containers such as pillow cases, drawstring bags, large boxes and crates.
- Ice-cube trays and sorting trays.
- Carts, trolleys, child size wheel barrows, pushchairs and prams.

Key words

- in, on and under
- empty, full, almost empty, almost full, brimming
- overflowing
- all gone, more and again
- in and out
- open and closed
- same and different

Connecting and disconnecting schemas in action

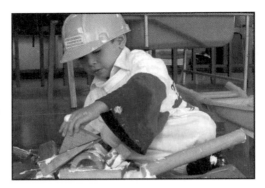

Definition: An interest in fastening and joining things together and in taking them apart. The schema can be seen in children's actions when they join train tracks, attach ropes to climbing frames, get fascinated with string and even tie their own legs together.

What happens?

Derrick and Mitchell are four and a half years old. They love connecting recycled household materials to make boats. Mitchell finds a long piece of wood, which he attaches to a smaller, narrower piece using nails, placing the small narrow piece of wood carefully in the centre on top of the long piece. Mitchell bangs in the nails to join the pieces together. He then hammers the two nails flat, so that they are bent over on to the wood and do not stick up. Mitchell takes his wooden model to the art area. Derrick is already there. He also has a construction of wood and recycled materials, including a cork and an empty yoghurt pot. Derrick has used glue to connect his wood together. Mitchell finds some glue and puts two dabs on top of his wood. He adds a cork and a shiny button. Mitchell says, 'Look, I've made a boat, like yours.' The boys then begin discussing their boats. They ask an adult if she can drill a hole in one end of their boat, so that they can fix on some string. The practitioner agrees to bring a drill into school the following day. Mitchell suggests that they try their boats out in the water tray. However, as Derrick and Mitchell approach the water tray, Derrick's boat falls apart. Mitchell helps him to fix the two pieces of wood together and they decide to let the glue dry first.

She brings the drill next day and helps the boys to drill the holes. Mitchell and Derrick attach string through the holes and go off to put their boats in the water tray. Mitchell watches as Derrick puts his boat in the shallow end of the water tray. 'It's not working,' he says to Derrick. Mitchell then puts his boat in. He tries it first in deeper water, where it floated. 'Where you are is where we should park our boats tonight,' he says to Derrick.

Again! Again!

What does this observation tell us?

This observation shows that connecting schemas have supported Mitchell and Derrick to think symbolically while making their boat models. Mitchell used nails to connect the parts of his boat together, and Derrick used glue. Mitchell is clearly using his prior knowledge and understanding about glue when he joins the wood together using nails. The underlying pattern running through their play is fastening and joining things.

> 'Children need to represent their experiences, their feelings, and ideas if they are to preserve them and share them with others. When we represent we make an object or symbol stand for something else.' *Bernadette Duffy*

> 'What a child can do with assistance today she will be able to do by herself tomorrow.'
> *Lev Vygotsky*

What do other babies and children do?

Babies and children may be interested in tying up kitchen or garden objects, joining toys together, fastening and joining things together using paper, tape, string and staples. Once children have explored the idea of connecting they often move on to separating or disconnecting things, like taking a wheel off a car or a head or leg off a doll. Toddlers tend to make connections with their bodies; for example, from about the age of two, a child may want to hold another's hand. At five, some children may want to swap clothes or shoes and handbags.

When young children first start to explore woodwork, they may be observed hammering lots of nails one after another into a piece of wood. In this activity they are likely to be problem solving and practising for themselves. Schemas are not only patterns of repeated actions, they link to children's existing knowledge, motivation, interests and preferences.

> 'Practitioners working in early education have a particularly important part to play in the search for understanding between the ages of two and five. These are the ages at which basic concepts are formed. Professional knowledge of 'continuity of learning' cannot fail to be furthered by knowledge of patterns of cognition in children under five in that knowledge of early learning illuminates later learning.' *Chris Athey*

The connecting and disconnecting schema

Definition: An interest in fastening and joining things together and in taking them apart. Children join train tracks, attach ropes to climbing frames, get fascinated with string and even tie their own legs together.

Some resources and activities

Construction

- Explore, build, weave with natural building materials, twigs, willow, raffia, dried grasses, corks and natural sponges, moss etc.
- Construct with hammer, nails, work bench, sandpaper, card, twine.
- Build bridges – mix regular construction toys, such as building bricks, with string, tape, magnets.
- Experiment with connecting with straws, sticky tape, paper clips, magnets, connecting sets.

Creative Play

- Try threading/jewelery making.
- Explore weaving and plaiting, with different textures and materials with different properties.
- Make paper chains.
- Build with junk materials, large and small.
- Provide tape, ribbons, string, elastic, cotton reels, bits of card and plastic.
- Use stick-on spots with junk box modelling.
- Making hanging mobiles, strings of flags and kites.

Messy play

- Investigate oil and water mixes in bottles, with paint or food colouring.
- Try pipes, tunnels and bridges in dry and wet sand.
- Add string and twisty tags to small objects in water play.
- Try cornflour and water gloop.
- Try runny paint patterns, making and diverting dribbles of paint to create maze-like pictures.
- Make connections in water play with pipes, hoses, funnels, jugs and buckets.

For inspiration

- Spiders' webs, scaffolding.
- Tube and road maps, atlases.
- Huge balls of string, wool rope, wool.

The treasure basket

- Treasury tags, pegs, rubber bands, lengths of string and ribbon, reels, tubes and other connecting objects.
- Key rings and paperclips, twisty tags and other fasteners, magnets, zips, toggles, threading toys

Again! Again!

Fine motor/creative

- Make human chains.
- Explore joins in construction, threading, sewing, weaving.
- Create train tracks and complex roadways.
- Make masking tape or chalk trails to follow.
- Build spiders' webs with thread in branches and twigs.
- Set up the dominoes to create a domino rally.
- Use string, tape, twisty tags to make trailers for cars and trains.
- Paper clip art with straws, sticky tape and big paper clips.
- Thread beads, pasta, polystyrene.

Outside

- Use large boxes and string to create trailers for wheeled toys.
- Weave lengths of natural or man-made materials through netting.
- Tie or weave fabric, ribbons, natural materials in fences and netting.
- Find a soft surface for some gentle three-legged races.
- Drill holes with a hand drill, make holes with a paper punch, use string, raffia and twine to join small pieces of wood or thin card.
- Make and use washing lines.
- Use string and paper to create runways, bridges and tunnels suspended from a climbing frame.
- Make mobiles in trees and bushes by hanging natural objects from strings or coat hangers.

Stories, rhymes & songs

- Ring games of all sorts - In and Out the Bluebells, Ring of Roses, The Mulberry Bush, The Hokey Cokey
- Line dancing.
- Partner games such as Row the Boat.
- Stories and rhymes such as Follow My Leader or One Elephant went out to Play.

Equipment to buy/find

- Fabrics, tapes, ribbon, string
- Clothes with fasteners
- Fasteners for making models, treasury tags, twisty tags, sticky tape, string, ribbon, elastic, cable ties, rope.
- Rubber bands and elastic.
- Offcuts of wood, tool bench, hinges, large screws, big nails.
- Everyday objects, such as clocks, locks to take apart.

Key words

- build, construct, join
- separate, open, close
- together, apart
- flexible, rigid
- heavy, light
- wood, plastic
- bendy, stretchy, strong, fragile
- tie, knot, thread
- stitch

Positioning schemas in action

Definition: An interest in carefully placing objects or themselves in patterns or rows. The schema may be seen when children line up toys, books or other objects and position them either on top, under, around the edge of, behind and next to each other.

What happens?

Fiona, aged four is arranging a selection of gemstones in an empty egg box. She covers the lid with pink tissue-paper, chooses some blue, green and purple gemstones and arranges them on the lid, positioning them on top, behind and next to one another. She gets a glue stick and some silver stars, and glues the stars round the edges of the lid, placing each star in a line, using her index finger as a spacer. She stands back and looks at her box, then she removes all the gemstones from the egg box and puts them back inside. She cuts out a rectangle of pink tissue-paper and glues it to the inside of the lid. Then she rearranges her gemstones in exactly the same position and glues them on to the top of the lid.

'Schemas are not just physical actions or skills but include ideas, concepts, bits of knowledge, verbal labels and so on.'   *Richard Gross*

What does this observation tell us?

Fiona has an interest in positioning objects in different places. Four of the stones were positioned upright. She shows her interest in what her artwork looks like from different viewpoints.

'Growth depends upon internalising events into a storage system that corresponds to the environment. It is this system that makes possible the child's increasing ability to go beyond the information encountered on a single occasion. He does this by making predictions and extrapolations from his stored model of the world.'   *Jerome Bruner*

Again! Again!

What do other babies and children do?

Other children can be observed positioning objects or themselves in a particular way, such as moving cars over and underneath bridges. Later children may be obsessed with positioning and will line up cars, trains and farm animals in order of size, colour and shape. They may be observed painting and creating collages, sticking scraps in sequence, placing materials in lines or painting or drawing with ordered lines. Older children may later produce drawings with missing elements and explain that something is behind the door or inside the handbag. This realisation that something can be behind the door or in the handbag and not visible is sometimes a new realisation as they are exploring with positioning.

> 'All schemas – both sensori-motor and cognitive – tend to be spontaneously applied or exercised. This provides the starting point for change – schemas will never change if they do not come into contact with new information.'
>
> Charles Brainerd

Some elements of the positioning schema may be difficult to cope with at home or in a setting, for example when a child constantly rearranges objects on shelves or in cupboards, insists on tidying up all the time, or stands on a supermarket trolley in a particular position. Parents and practitioners need to find alternative ways to allow the child to fully explore their schema, because the schema will drive behaviour anyway, and they will pursue the schemas regardless of whether practitioners or parents approve. Schema exploration allows children to develop a sense of worth and pride in themselves as well as motivating them to learn, explore and discover more.

> 'Allowing children to pursue their schema can be seen as respecting how they become interested, excited and motivated.'
>
> Lillian Katz and Sylvia Chard

The positioning schema

Definition: An interest in placing objects or themselves in patterns or rows. The schema may be seen when children line up toys, books or other objects and position them either on top, under, around the edge of, behind and next to each other.

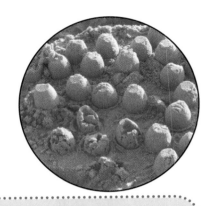

Some resources and activities

Children with this schema love to sort and put objects on top of something, on the edge, all round and behind other objects.

You might see children with this schema:

- stacking unlikely objects;
- lining up toys;
- creating layers in paint or collage;
- balancing objects on the edges of shelves or tables;
- working with small objects and activities with multiple pieces.

Again! Again!

Children with this schema may enjoy:
- creating elaborate frames for pictures;
- sorting small objects;
- making mosaics with collage materials;
- making pictures with shapes;
- using peg boards to create patterns and shapes;
- magnetic or wooden mosaics for patterns and pictures;
- games involving hiding and finding objects.

Key words
- inside
- on top
- under
- behind
- between
- next to
- in front

Orientation schemas in action

Definition: An interest in seeing things from different angles. Children hang upside down from the slide or climbing frame and may turn their toys and objects upside down as they look at them.

What happened?

Jasper, aged four years, is hanging upside down on the top of a garden slide. He slides down head first. Later the practitioner observes him running up the slide. He does this several times, until he is told to stop by the practitioner because it could have been dangerous. The practitioner suggests that Jasper finds a way of climbing up the slide other than running up. Jasper begins to climb up the slide slowly holding on to the outer edges; he lowers his body to aid his balance and grips on using his arms to pull his body up. In this way it takes Jasper very little time to reach the top. Then he tries to turn his body around but loses his balance and ends up sliding down on his tummy. The practitioner observes that Jasper appears to enjoy it. He climbs the slide again and, on reaching the top, he tries again to turn on to his back but only manages to slide down again on his tummy. Despite not being able to rotate on to his back, Jasper takes great enjoyment from sliding down on his front.

What does this observation tell us?

In this observation Jasper uses the top of the slide as a place to see his surroundings from a different viewpoint. He experiments with movement and orientation. He has good coordination and is able to solve the problem of climbing the slide by doing it in an imaginative way. In addition, he is able to practise new moves. The practitioner makes a judgement that running up the slide may expose Jasper to danger, while recognising his needs to extend his play.

'Good supervision is essential and we should aim to allow children some freedom, but adults must also help children to know their limitations and the consequences of their actions.'   *Penny Tassoni and Karen Tucker*

Again! Again!

'Encourage independence as young children explore, particularly patterns of movement, sometimes referred to as schemas.'   *EYFS*

What do other babies and children do?

Orientation play takes place as babies and young children move around. They need movement to strengthen their muscles as they gain control of their heads, arms, hands, feet and legs. Babies will often be observed wiggling their bodies furiously. When babies lie on their tummies or backs, sit up, crawl, stand, walk, and travel in a car or buggy, they will begin to see the world from a different perspective. When a baby with a strong orientation schema starts to crawl they can be observed manoeuvring their bodies backwards across obstacles and down stairs with great confidence and coordination. Others may be observed crawling on the grass on hands and knees, then raising themselves on to hands and feet when crawling on the gravel path.

'The most important factors for healthy development are that you should recognise the skills a child has developed and provide plenty of opportunitieto practise them.'   *Tina Bruce and Carolyn Meggitt*

'Respect individual preoccupations, allow time to explore and practise movements.'   *Curriculum Guidance for the Foundation Stage*

The orientation schema

Definition: An interest in seeing things from different angles. Children hang upside down from the slide or climbing frame and may turn their toys and objects upside down as they look at them.

Some resources and activities

Children with this schema love to look at things from different angles.

You might see children with this schema:

- turn things upside down to look at them;
- examine the underneath of objects;
- hang upside down to observe other children playing;
- bend to look at the world from different directions, including between their own legs.

Children with this schema may enjoy:

- kaleidoscopes;
- mirror play;
- magnifying lenses;
- binoculars;
- creating peep holes;
- posting boxes.

Again! Again!

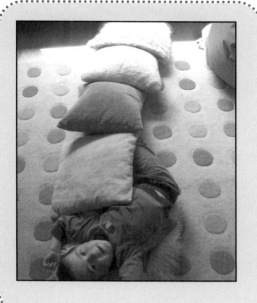

Children invoved in this schema may enjoy:

- pendulums;
- moving like animals to music or poems;
- climbing, swinging;
- ropes and tyre swings;
- tumbling mats and headstands;
- low bars to swing and hang from and roll over;
- mirrors in unusual places such as on the floor or the ceiling.

When children are out of doors, provide plenty of opportunities to roll, tumble, climb, twist and spin.

Key words

- turn
- upside down
- backwards
- over
- twist
- roll
- under

Supporting schema play

References

Athey, Chris. (1990) Extending Thoughts in Young Children: A Parent-Teacher Partnership; Paul Chapman

Sheridan, Mary. (1975) Children's Developmental Progress from Birth to Five Years: Stycar Sequences; NFER Publishing, Slough

DCSF. (2007) Early Years Foundation Stage

Minett, Pamela. (1985) Child Care & Development; John Murray Publishing

Matthews, John. (2003) Drawing and Painting: Children and Visual Representation; Paul Chapman Publishing.

Papert, Seymour. (2005) Mind Storms: Children, Computers, and Powerful Ideas; Harvester Press, 1980 in Early Childhood Education, 3rd Edition, Hodder Arnold, 2005

Nutbrown, Cathy. (2006) Threads of Thinking, Young Children and the Role of Early Education; 3rd Edition; Sage Publications.

Whitehead, Marion. (2002) Developing Language and Literacy with Young Children; Paul Chapman.

Lev Vygotsky. (1978) Minds in Society; Harvard University Press

Bruce, Tina. (1987/2005) Early Childhood Education; Hodder & Stoughton.

Lindon Jennie. (2001) Understanding Children's Play; Nelson Thornes.

Nutbrown, Cathy. (1998) Threads of Thinking, Young Children Learning and the Role of Early Years Educators; Paul Chapman

Kilton, Neil. (1994) The Excellence of Play; Open University Press.

Davis, Mollie. (2003) Movement and Dance in Early Childhood; Paul Chapman

Duffy, Bernadette. (1998) Supporting Creativity and Imagination in the Early Years; Open University Press

Vygotsky, Lev. (1962) Thought and Language; Wiley & Sons.

Tassoni, Penny and Tucker, Karen. (2000) Planning Play and the Early Years; Heinemann

Bruce, Tina and Meggitt Carolyn. (2002) Child Care & Education; Hodder & Stoughton.

QCA (2000) Curriculum Guidance for the Foundation Stage; Department for Education and Skills.

Gross, Richard (2005) Psychology: The Science of Mind and Behaviour; Hodder & Stoughton.

Bruner, Jerome. (1967) Towards a Theory of Instruction; Harvard University Press

Brainerd, Charles. (1978) Piaget's Theory of Intelligence; Prentice-Hall

Again! Again!

More than one schema

This chapter explores the situations where children become involved in multiple schemas, sometimes, two, sometimes more. Many experts believe that schema play in most children occurs in multiples.

Sometimes babies and young children display more than one schema in their play and explorations, and when this is observed, the result is usually referred to as a cluster of schemas. Among the most influential research into schemas and schema clusters was thatundertaken in new Zealand by Anne Meade and Pam Cubey in 1995. Funded by the New Zealand Council for Education Research, they investigated schemas and schema clusters in children aged three to five years, and published their findings in a book called *Thinking Children*.

They wanted to explore whether schemas operated in isolation, one at a time, in sequence, and their research findings provided early years practitioners with a revised perspective on schematic development. Before this research it was believed that individual schemas dominated children's development for a period of time, but the study revealed that schemas often work in pairs and groups to form a network of clusters, rising and falling, grouping and re-grouping as the child's learning and interests change.

'Schema clusters seem at times to rise and dominate what the child does, and at other times it is as if they have gone into hibernation.' Tina Bruce

The research also revealed the importance of the context of the child's learning - human interactions and social and cultural aspects appeared to have a significant impact on the development and coordination of schema clusters. As children develop, their schema clusters begin to function together, enabling the child to think and act at much higher levels than they would with just one schema.

For example, when the trajectory schema is part of a cluster of schemas, thinking and action may be concentrated on lines - up, down or side-to-side - and dabs. Once a child has explored horizontal and vertical lines separately, they often move on to use the lines together to form crosses, grids, diagonals or zigzags. A schema cluster may then appear, as they begin to coordinate lines into enclosures. The continuing activity and the thinking involved produces much more complex networks of connections in the brain.

'Whilst young children can sometimes be observed paying attention to a particular schema, older children's learning involves coordination of schemas. Coordination and connection mark important progression in learning at all stages where combinations and co-ordinations of schemas develop into higher-order concepts.'   Cathy Nutbrown

'Core and radial' is a description used when children construct, draw or paint representations with a central part or point from which radial objects or lines extend. This often occurs when children who are exploring a rotational schema find the connection between trajectories and enclosures. Core and radial features can often be recognised in children's drawings and paintings as:

     a head with hair;

     fingers and toes;

     rainbows;

     flowers with petals;

     spiders with legs;

     eyelashes;

     a sun with rays.

Younger children may begin by making scribbles such as up and down strokes and circular scribbles. They then go on to explore dots, dabs and straight lines before they start to enclose, connect and cover up their marks.

Understanding what this schema looks like in practice and how dynamic it is may provide a valuable tool for practitioners, especially when planning activities for individuals and small groups. Practitioners can become actively involved in talking through the connections that children are making, providing a range of materials to encourage experimentation and recording the learning taking place.

'Schemas are patterns of linked behaviours which the child can generalise and use in a whole variety of different situations. It is best to think of schemas as being a cluster of pieces, which fit together.' Tina Bruce

Practitioners may decide to make use of these observations to construct and resource individual activity plans, using the schemas they are observing.

Other clusters of schemas will appear as children begin to link their ideas and thinking into longer chains of brain connections. These include combining trajectory and connecting, transporting and filling, transforming and enclosing etc. The following examples show combined schemas in action.

Again! Again!

Core and radial graphic

> Joy and Alice, aged five, draw human figures with radial lines coming out of their navels, saying these radials are belly tattoos.

Trajectory and connecting

> Jack, aged five, is observed connecting pieces of wood together. He has joined pieces of wood together in a stepped, zigzag way. The practitioner observes Jack hammering in ten nails to connect the difficult join. Jack then hammers each nail in so the heads are totally flat.

Transporting and infilling

> Alison, aged three, has a fascination for anything that can be pushed, such as prams, trolleys and wheel barrows. She is also very interested in carrying a bag or basket wherever she goes. The practitioner observes Alison filling her bag with a variety of objects, which she carries from place to place around the room. Later, she is observed being selective about what is being pushed or carried and has begun to match items to the particular roles she is acting out, such as the doll in the pram is taken out by mum, the letters and envelope in her bag are for the postman.

Enveloping and infilling

> Tia, aged four, enjoys dressing up, putting on hats, shoes and carrying her handbags filled with bits and pieces. The childminder observes her starting to make lots of parcels, big and small. She is observed taking boxes and filling them with bits of paper. She wraps her boxes and tubes of paper using masking tape.

Transforming and enclosing

> Serena and Stacy Ann, both aged four, are observed mixing paints to make pink, green and purple colours. They pour their mixtures into bottles which they seal with paper and tape.

Rotation and orientation

> Adam, aged three, is playing inside a big cardboard box in the nursery garden. He rotates himself round and round inside the box, saying, 'I go round and round'. Then he fetches a broom, gets back in his box and, holding it by the brush end, turns it round and says 'I'm coming to get you'.

More than one schema

As you will see, spotting, observing, recording and unravelling complex clusters of schemas can be difficult. Practitioners may wish to ensure a flexible response to children by recognising that schematic behaviour can be complex, and that there is usually a reason for what may seem puzzling behaviour that they witness and record as they observe the babies and young children in their care.

Ongoing observation and assessment of babies' and young children's actions, interests and development is an integral part of the practitioner's role. It informs them of what to plan and provide for children to extend their developing interests.

The original *Birth to Three Matters Guidance* introduced us all to the notion of 'Look, listen and note'. Trying to observe and write notes at the same time is difficult, even for practiced observers, and the focus on only writing what is useful is more difficult still. The *Birth to Three Matters Guidance* suggested that practitioners should look first, then listen, then (after a pause for thought) note the important things they have seen.

Practitioners need to develop and refine their observation skills so they can quickly and helpfully note babies' and young children's schemas. Toddlers may be observed repeating an action again and again, such as climbing up and down low steps, or walking on low walls. Between the age of around 18 months to two years, children begin to represent their schematic actions in their play with everyday objects. For example, they may start to rotate their bowl pretending that they are steering a car. This is called symbolic representation and marks a significant and important developmental stage when children are able to use one object to stand for another (a baby brush for a hairbrush, leaves or stones for money, a box for a boat). And from about three and a half years children may be observed using what Tina Bruce calls 'Functional Dependency' (turning the cooker on in their pretend play because they have observed that it needs to be on in order to cook).

Notes should be made of babies' reactions to being shown different objects and how they respond to games such as Peek-a-boo. The observations should record babies' interest in reaching for and grasping objects, how they use their senses and movements to explore, which toys excite them most, and what attachments they make with different people. All these things produce valuable information about the baby's learning and development.

'Close observation of young children at play suggests that they find out about the world in the same way scientists explore new phenomena and test new ideas. Young children may not be able to verbalise new ideas forming in their heads, but may still apply similar processes to objects and events through simple, if crude, scientific investigation.'   Jillian Roden

Again! Again!

A key part of the practitioner's role is to observe children so they can:
- find out about the child's interests and schemas;
- recognise their stages of development;
- identify their preferred learning styles;
- plan for all areas of learning and for experiences that may not arise every day.

'The more the teacher learns about the understanding of individuals, the more effectively he or she will be able to select appropriate curriculum content for both individuals and groups.'   *Chris Athey*

When recording observations, practitioners should write down what they see and hear, not what they think. Not every detail will need to be recorded, but they should take care to describe non-verbal communication and make a record of relevant spoken words. They should wait until they have completed the observation before asking themselves 'What seems to be significant, new or different in terms of the child's learning and development?'

Observations enable practitioners to:
- understand and value babies' and young children's learning and development;
- respect children's unique differences;
- build on what children already know, and extend their interest in language and thinking;
- plan dynamic, challenging and interactive play experiences to sustain and extend thinking;
- work in partnership with parents, carers and other professionals.

Practitioners need to understand that they and the learning environment play a key role in supporting and extending babies' and young children's learning and development. For example, a child exploring covering their hands and fingers with paint will need practitioners who can support their learning by providing a range of other materials for covering themselves and objects. The learning environment has a powerful influence on children's development, as it 'speaks' to them and they are interpreting what it says all the time. A rich and stimulating environment will support the emergence of schemas, and will ensure that babies and children have the resources they need to pursue their schematic play.

Again! Again!

Look, listen and note

As soon as they can talk, young children ask questions all the time - 'how? what? why? and when?' - as they talk or sign. Observation of children's play enables practitioners to ask children questions based on their actions and any symbolic representation that may have been observed. Sensitive questioning enables the practitioner to understand what the child is thinking, as well as helping the child to extend their ideas.

'Build on children's particular interests by adding resources to sustain and extend their efforts.'   Early Years Foundation Stage (EYFS)

'The importance of the schema is that it provides a mechanism for analysing 'where the child is' and helps to predict other situations that will be of interest to the child.'   Tina Bruce

> Nathaniel, aged four, is playing a game of road works with a group of other children. He works with the group to collect and transport crates, move A frames and planks and create an enclosed space. He then gets some black sugar paper and places single sheets of it in a long line in the centre of his enclosure. Nathaniel then takes one of the other children into the garden with him. They return with stones and grass, which they place on the sugar paper. 'We have dig a hole,' Nathaniel told the practitioner.

Here is a list of questions, based on this observation of Nathaniel, that practitioners could ask themselves relating to Nathaniel's interests:

What ideas is Nathaniel currently exploring?

What schemas or clusters of schemas did he follow?

What first hand experience has he had which led him to developing an interest in 'road works'?

What might you discuss with his parents about his interests (would you use photos of Nathaniel in action)?

What activities and resources are you going to plan to offer on following days to extend his thinking?

Which other children might you involve in these future activities and why?

How will you know if the new resources and activities have been successful?

Could you plan an adult-initiated activity that will extend Nathaniel's knowledge about road works?

'Observing and identifying schemas allows practitioners to make sense of what some children are doing so that behaviour which for example seems to lack concentration, might show itself to have a clear methodology after all.'
Marjorie Ouvry

'All planning starts with observing children in order to understand and consider their current interests, development and learning.'
EYFS

Tina Bruce in her book a 'Time to Play' provides practitioners with twelve features of free-flow play and active learning that practitioners could use when assessing or evaluating young children involved in self-chosen experiences or activities:

1. Free-flow play is an active process without a product.

2. Free-flow play is intrinsically motivated.

3. Free-flow play exerts no external pressure to conform to rules, pressures, goals, tasks or definite directions.

4. Free-flow play is about possible alternative worlds, which involve 'supposing' and 'as if' which lift players to their highest level of functioning. This involves being imaginative, original, innovative and creative.

5. Free-flow play is about participants wallowing in ideas, feelings and relationships. It involves, reflecting on and becoming aware of what we know, or 'metacognition'.

6. Free-flow play actively uses previous first-hand experiences, including struggle, manipulation, exploration, discovery and practice.

7. Free-flow play is sustained and, when in full flow, helps us to function in advance of what we can actually do in our real lives.

8. During free-flow play we use the technical prowess and competency we have previously developed, and so we can be in control.

9. Free-flow play can be initiated by a child or an adult, but if by the adult he/she must pay particular attention to Features 3,5, and 11.

10. Free-flow play can be solitary.

11. Free-flow play can be in partnerships, or groups of adults and/or children, who will be sensitive to each other.

12. Free-flow play is an integrating mechanism, which brings together everything we learn, know, feel and understand.

Tina Bruce

Again! Again!

Practitioners will need to develop an understanding of the features and language of free-flow play. Knowledge of these features will support them in gaining a valuable insight into children's levels of interest and what motivates them.

'The basis of good teaching is informed observation.' Tina Bruce

Some different ways of assessing learning

There are many different ways of observing and recording what babies and children are doing and learning. Some of the most commonly used are:

1. **Sampled observations of individual children**. These will give practitioners an accurate picture of what children have achieved over a period of time and in different situations.

2. **Using a digital tape recorder** is a good way to measure progress of language and communication.

3. **Checklists** will provide a simple overview of development. Practitioners should only use checklists if they already have a good working knowledge of the child, as they can give an over-simplified view.

4. Targeting **key children** will enable practitioners to focus on a particular interest or schema, or on one child over different activities and observed by different adults.

5. **Written narrative observations**, noting everything a child does over a short period of time, will enable practitioners to record significant steps in learning and development.

6. **Learning diaries** can be used by practitioners daily and taken home to share with parents. This will give children an opening to reflect on their own achievements with parents and practitioners.

7. **Anecdotal notes** will assist practitioners to record children's spontaneous learning and development.

8. **Photographs, video and tape recordings** of children talking are excellent (but more time-consuming) ways to help practitioners confirm findings of observations gained using other methods.

The EYFS promotes a play based philosophy. It emphasises the 'uniqueness' of every child's learning journey and promotes ongoing assessment of children's play as an integral part of the learning and development process. It states that early years practitioners should:

> Make systematic observations and assessments of each child's achievements, interest and learning styles;

> Use observation and assessment to identify learning priorities and plan

---

Look, listen and note

relevant and motivating learning experiences for each child.

'Providers must ensure that practitioners are observing children and responding appropriately to help them make progress from birth towards the early learning goals.'   EYFS

Practitioners need to be able to plan and resource learning experiences to extend and support play and active learning. The following examples provide practitioners with a template for observing, following up what they see, and providing resources:

What the practitioner saw

I saw Sacha, aged 15 months, holding and turning a cotton reel. She poked her fingers into the hole at the end of the cotton reel. Then she turned it round and round on her finger and let it drop off. I think this is a rotational schema.

Follow up activity suggested by the practitioner

Sing the nursery rhyme 'Wind the Bobbin Up' with actions; then provide a long cardboard tube and ping-pong balls to roll or drop through it.

Resources to add

Cardboard tube, ping-pong balls.

What the practitioner saw

Olivia, 26 months, kept walking and running round and round the little flower tub in the nursery garden.

Follow up activity suggested by the practitioner

Next time I see Olivia doing this activity, I'll join her and sing nursery rhymes such as 'Round and Round the Garden', 'Here we go Round the Mulberry Bush', and "Round and Round the Village'. I could also take a CD player and a nursery rhyme CD outside, and offer her a chiffon scarf for waving round and round.

Resources to provide

CD player and CDs, chiffon scarves.

Again! Again!

What the practitioner saw

Greg, 30 months, was using his index finger to make patterns in the dry sand.

Follow up activity suggested by the practitioner

We will offer finger painting and foam play in the creative area over the next few days and watch how Greg responds.

Resources to add

Finger paints, foam. Add cotton buds later.

What the practitioner saw

Moira, 36 months, was filling a bag with all the cooking utensils from the home play area. She took these outside and tipped them out on the picnic rug. Then she collected them all again and brought them back.

Follow up activity suggested by the practitioner

Add some different sorts of bags and containers to the home play - purses, shopping bags, little baskets, envelopes, and some dry pasta and other items to fill them with. We could also make a shop.

Resources to add

More baskets and other containers. Dry pasta, beans, real vegetables etc.

Good practice tips for observing and recording learning and development at

---

What the practitioner saw

Taylor, 46 months, is fascinated with the link between the new tractor and trailer. He constantly joins and disconnects it, only driving the tractor a few feet before getting off to disconnect the trailer and fix it on again. He spent nearly half an hour in this sort of play.

Follow up activity suggested by the practitioner

We could remind Taylor about the magnetic train set, the car racing track and the marble run, by putting these somewhere obvious and showing the whole group where they are. We could also use these in group time to make sure all the children know how they fit together. Perhaps Taylor could demonstrate!

Resources to add

Train and car tracks, marble run (do we need some more marbles?).

Look, listen and note

What the practitioner saw

Tom, 22 months, was climbing on and off an armchair. Later he was seen standing on top of one of the ride-along cars and then stacking cushions one on top of the other to see how high he could make the pile.

Follow up activity suggested by the practitioner

I will read the Anansi story, and talk about the different ways spiders move, then offer some boxes and ladders to climb up.

Resources to add

'A' frames, ladders, boxes.

What the practitioner saw

Kea, four months, was sitting observing other children with her thumb in her mouth, rubbing her blanket. This may be the start of a trajectory schema.

Follow up activity suggested by the practitioner

I will offer Kea some furry fabric and shiny and crinkly paper in a basket beside her.

Resources needed

Furry fabric, shiny and crinkly paper.

What the practitioner saw

Hitesh, aged nine months, was sitting on the floor playing with six soft cubes. He examined them with both hands, put them his mouth and sucked them. He repeatedly lifted the cubes up one at a time, held his arms up high and then dropped them.

Follow up activity suggested by the practitioner

We will offer Hitesh a follow-up activity - a basket of soft balls, bean bags and other soft objects for him to grasp, squeeze, throw, drop.

Resources needed

Plastic and rubber balls of various sizes, ping-pong balls, bean bags.

Again! Again!

each of the six development stages are identified in the EYFS Practitioner Guidance and on the good practice cards:

To help children progress practitioners need information about what the children know, understand and can do. Through observing children and by making notes when necessary about what has been achieved, practitioners can make professional judgements about children's achievements and decide on the next steps in learning. They can also exchange information with parents about how children are progressing. This process, often known as 'assessment for learning' is central to raising achievement.   *EYFS*

Watching children as they play, devising a simple way of recording what you see, and using this information to plan additions, offers and small group activities, will ensure you are building on what children already know and can do, taking them to Vygotsky's:

'... zone of proximal development - the difference between the child's capacity to solve problems independently and the capacity to solve problems with assistance from an adult.'

References

Rodd, Jill. (1994) <u>Leadership in Early Years; The Pathway to Professionalism</u>

Athey, Chris. (1990) <u>Extending Thought in Young Children; A Teacher Parent Partnership</u>; Paul Chapman

DCSF. (2007) <u>Statutory Framework and Practitioner Guidance on the Early Years Foundation Stage</u>

Bruce, Tina. (1969) <u>A Time to Play In Early Childhood Education</u>; Hodder & Stoughton

Ouvry, Marjorie. (2005) <u>Exercising Muscles and Minds: Outdoor Play and the Early Years Curriculum</u>; National Children's Bureau

Hutchin, Vicky. (2003) <u>Observing and Assessing for the Foundation Stage Profile</u>; Hodder Murray

DCFS. (May 2008) <u>Early Years Foundation Stage Statutory Framework and Practitioner Guidance</u>

Again! Again!

Using observations of schemas in planning

Incorporating observations of children's play in planning next steps is a familiar procedure in the early years. Adding information about current schemas is less commonly seen. In this chapter, two practitioners explain the way they plan, using schema play as well as children's current interests.

Liz Magraw and Lisa Hayes, a head teacher and deputy head team, created a very special place in the centre of Nottingham. Merrivale was a Local Authority (LA) maintained nursery school in a truly urban setting. Literally thousands of cars and lorries thundered by over a nearby flyover creating high levels of traffic noise and pollution, but in a far from ideal location an oasis was created. As a result of the reorganisation of education in the LA, the nursery has now closed, and the children have been dispersed to other provision in the area.

Merrivale nursery was more than the physical building. It developed a small, highly interactive and constantly changing outdoor space, complete with a music area, teepee, sensory garden, rope bridges, a tree house, a camouflaged 'dark' shed, movable theatre staging, a willow tunnel, a patch to grow fruit, vegetables and herbs, and much more. But what made Merrivale such a special place was that the children planned their own spaces, indoors and outdoors, and how they were used, acting as leaders in the development of each part of the environment. This planning was supported through observation and consideration of the children's schemas.

The children spent a session every week in woodland, experiencing a wide range of adult and child-led forest activities. However, even off site the children were central to the planning and review of the all the activities.

In this section, Liz and Lisa explore the value of planning for and from schemas, and explore the possibilities for extending this method further. They give a step-by-step explanation of how to plan from schemas, and how to review and evaluate the resulting work. They also reflect on how planning through schemas has enabled them to develop their practice in meeting the needs of all children, including those with special needs.

Schemas and planning as described by Liz and Lisa

The decision to use schemas as part of our planning evolved from the process of reviewing and evaluating the quality and effectiveness of our practice. We recognised that we tended to plan too many adult-led activities to enable us to make relevant and useful observations of children's learning. So as part of the process of striving to improve personalised learning for children, we decided as a staff team to use schemas for planning the provision made for all children at Merrivale. We felt strongly that this would enable us to focus more clearly on and identify individual children's learning patterns.

After much team discussion and careful consideration, we decided to refocus the provision to enable adults to:

- establish and commit to maintaining a daily free-flow between indoors and out of doors;
- make more high quality observations;
- undertake more in-depth interventions;
- further support the extension of children's ideas.

We also aimed to focus observations so they provided the quality and detail of information needed to extend children's learning and to support the planning process.

What we did

All the staff were already familiar with and had a strong understanding of brain based learning and learning styles. They had considered each child's preferred learning style and had, in particular, identified visual, auditory and kinaesthetic learners. Further support was provided to enable staff to discover and understand their own learning style and how this impacts on their teaching style.

We also recognised that using children's schemas would help us achieve our goal of providing holistic, inclusive practice which enhanced personalised learning through a development of independence, with children directing their own learning, having the confidence and autonomy to take their learning forward and scaffolding their own learning. The adult therefore took the role of 'pedagogue' (a word adopted more recently to describe a teacher who works as a learning partner with the children), relinquishing the more traditional role of teacher as instructor.

We wanted to ensure that inclusion was deeply rooted in our practice, in every aspect of learning and teaching, so all children were given access to learning

Again! Again!

that would support development in all areas - for example they had regular opportunities to do yoga, experience interactive music and sound awareness and EASIE (Exercise and Sound in Education).

This commitment did not result in a 'one size fits all' system. Opportunities were provided, children accessed them at their own stage of learning and were targeted accordingly by the adults. As with any change, our new methods required full commitment from all staff, and through an appropriate programme of training, the knowledge and confidence of all staff grew, enhancing the cohesion and spirit of the staff team. We started the process by looking together in depth at the characteristics of effective learning and teaching, relating this back to our existing practice and the way we work.

Our reading and research included the works of Ferre Laever, Vivian Gussain Paley, Howard Gardner, Alistair Smith, Daniel Goleman, Te Whariki, Daniel Hughes and Chris Athey. These references were all influential in finding direction for our thoughts and aspirations. We were also deeply engaged in the Forest School movement, which had a huge impact on our approach. The Primary Strategy: *Excellence and Enjoyment* published by DfES in 2003 (DfES 0377/2003) reinforced our thinking.

Schemas and short term planning

While consideration was given to schemas when preparing long and medium term plans, it was in the weekly short-term planning that schemas took the lead. The whole staff were involved in the planning, so everyone had an understanding of the process, the content, their role in it and the purpose for the children's learning. Each weekly plan was informed by the medium-term plans, by children's reviews and by staff observations and assessments done throughout the previous week.

The children's involvement at this stage was crucial. In the children's reviews, each child could talk about what they had done and analyse their learning, including what they had not taken part in or succeeded in. The children themselves qualified what they said and began to think of a solution, a way forward. These reviews took place every Thursday in key groups and the adults recorded the children's comments. Reviews were followed by a staff planning session at the end of Thursday, referring to these review notes, which were also published for parents to see each week.

The planning meeting

We began each planning meeting by deciding on adult-led activities and their objectives, ensuring that there was an even spread across all areas of learning, across levels and throughout the week. Finer differentiation took place during the activity through staff in-depth knowledge of each child's learning style.

We allocated each activity to members of staff, again ensuring that the staff worked across a spread of activities and areas of learning to offer a variety of presentation and learning styles to the children. Each day, there were at least two adult 'buddies' (floating support) who had the crucial role of:

supporting the children's well-being, involvement and learning;

assisting them in their personal care if required;

encouraging them to engage and socialise wherever it was needed.

The children knew that the buddies were there to support them, helping them to develop strategies rather than enforcing rules. Each day, children enthusiastically took it in turn to be a buddy too, learning to lead, and discovering the responsibilities that come with leadership. It was a much sought-after position.

The short-term plans also included small group activities and their objectives. The aim of our small (key) group work was to develop Personal, Social and Emotional Development, although the content of each activity might lie in any area of learning. As these groups were key person groups, the children remained affiliated to the same group throughout their time at the nursery, building strong relationships both with their peers and with the adult who was their key person, the one who would write their settling-in report. Weekly off-site visits to forest settings were also integrated into planning at this stage.

The focus children, targeted for visual and written observations each day, were also noted in the planning. There was a rotation within each group of children observed daily to ensure that all children were observed over a period of time, and a minimum of six children were specifically targeted each day by all the adults in order to ensure a breadth of viewpoints. On occasion, individuals might be chosen because of our concerns, and more extensive observations of these children would be conducted, or a member of staff would add an observation about a child not originally selected if they felt we might miss relevant and important information.

As the week progressed, the plans were evaluated and adjusted to respond to the way the activities were developing or to children's comments and engagement. This ensured that planning was adjusted to meet the children's needs immediately or a note was made on the planning sheet to inform the next planning session.

Alongside the adult-led activities, on-going activities were also planned. From experience, we devised the headings we felt were the most appropriate for the

Again! Again! —

spread of skills that develop in young children and for a wide range of opportunities. See page 100 for a sample planning sheet.

Adding the schemas

Over five weeks, the planning covered five schemas: connecting, transporting, trajectory, rotation and enveloping. After some deliberation, we realised that between them, these five schemas broadly covered all possible angles of schematic learning and formed a good starting point. Each week, activities were planned under most headings with a focus on one of the schemas. On week six the children planned the on-going activities in their review time, and this inevitably gave a good mixture of all five schemas.

We put together a list of schema-dominant activities, ideas, resources to help the process of planning and to inspire staff in developing ideas and in analysing the nature of activities in schematic terms (see page 101).

We tried to ensure that there was a balance between adult-led and ongoing activities in terms of skills, areas of learning and levels. The ongoing activities generally remained the same throughout the week, though they were often positioned differently, indoors and/or out of doors, front or back of the nursery etc. This was to make sure that all children, whatever their inclination, preferred learning style, or dominant schema, had the opportunity to access them. The involvement of an adult, particularly the buddy, also encouraged children to become involved.

Both adult-led and ongoing activities alternated between indoors and outdoors with a complete free-flow between outside and inside, activities taking place anywhere. Outside and inside are of equal importance; so, for instance, climbing could be indoors, painting and writing could be set up outside; access to the outside was not weather dependent because every child had a waterproof and wellies, and quickly became competent in dressing and undressing. When there was a lot of rain, we also used tarpaulins to protect activities such as painting. However, you soon realise how little it really rains throughout the year, and we probably used tarpaulin covers more in the summer as sun protection! The children got so used to flowing freely that they naturally and independently moved between indoors and outdoors. Children are seldom discouraged by the weather, do not complain about it, and indeed, get very excited about weather changes. On a rainy day, recently, a mum told us that her daughter was looking forward to splashing in puddles with her friends.

We found that planning needed to be flexible and open to adaptation at any time. Depending on the children's input, activities may be altered, moved on or completely abandoned if or when the children express a different interest, introduce a new aspect or decide to extend an existing interest further. For instance, if children are fully involved in planning and making imaginative areas, they decide what they are going to make and where they are going to position it. They draw plans, decide on materials required and construction methods as they build it, getting involved in decision-making, team-work and problem-solving.

We monitored all short-term planning every six weeks for coverage of all the curriculum clusters and their stages. Some curriculum aspects such as self care fit more easily in the medium-term planning, since they are of a continuous nature. The medium-term planning showed how these objectives can be met, how the setting was organised to enable children to achieve these goals and how adults supported it. We found numerous benefits in incorporating schemas in our planning. Some that we were expecting, others which we were not.

We expected medium and short-term planning that incorporated schemas to:

- help us diagnose children's dominant schemas faster, **but** we also found that it impacted on all our observations making them more focussed and more effective;
- provide more coalescent on-going planning **but** it also impacted very quickly on planning for adult-led activities, giving more continuity and solidity to the whole planning content and process. In fact, it influenced our whole approach and ethos;
- give us a format to improve differentiation **but** it became more than this and fits in perfectly with our personalised learning approach. It is a really useful and natural base from which to analyse learning and move it forward. It also proved to be a really useful tool to support children on the autistic spectrum;
- support our Forest School approach which is central to our outdoor learning ethos.

The weekly focus on one schema helped to define each child's dominant schema(s) if they had any, but also their tendencies and interests if they did not have a particularly dominant schema. Differentiation created by planning for a different schema each week highlighted a child's tendency but also revealed whether they were struggling with any other kind of schematic play.

Leon is a pure transporter. He has to be moving something his hands. He is also very specific about the object he holds, ideally a blue bus, but failing this, any play vehicle. His play focus is to move items of his choice from their original position to another. Nothing is ever where you expect it to be with Leon about. He is possessive about what he is transporting, often hiding it to ensure that nobody else can take possession or can move it elsewhere. He gets distraught if he is unable to do this.

These observations have given us an understanding of why Leon is rarely settling on one activity unless it is a typically 'transporting' activity. Observations have made us understand why he is obsessed about certain toys, what he does with them and why he is at a complete loss when they are not available.

Some strategies based on these observations have been successful with Leon. We have ensured that toys he favours are available, but in different situations and locations, as an incentive to bring his interest to other activities. We have given concentrated intervention in providing for his needs while introducing him to new opportunities. Leon is beginning to communicate his needs rather than hitting others (a regular occurrence if they touched his favoured toy).

He is beginning to listen and negotiate, although adults still need to talk with him before a certain point of 'no return' when he is so upset about the loss of a favourite object that he can no longer accept either physical reassurance or verbal communication. He is beginning to talk to other children in his play.

Part of his protective behaviour shows elements of enveloping. However through all these developments, he has begun to show strengths in becoming a connector, especially through his mental processes. For instance, he is now particularly applying pieces of knowledge learnt in one situation to others and correlating them to strengthen his learning and to expand his interests.

The weekly focus on one of the five identified schemas encouraged children to explore schemas that did not come naturally to them, therefore providing possibilities that might otherwise not have presented themselves. Observing the children's interaction with activities, whether with their dominant schema or not, helped us identify ways forward in their learning.

Suki came to nursery as a pure enveloper, with some of the worries that can be attached to this schema, particularly the need to bring something from home, to carry it around everywhere, and to become distraught if she loses it. She also felt more comfortable in small, enclosed and cosy areas. Another typical behaviour was to black out a picture once drawn or painted, and this is something which can cause anxiety in adults. Suki's behaviour made her parents feel very concerned, thinking that there was a more sinister explanation. Now they have an understanding of her schema they can cope with it and even be positive, encouraging her to talk and certainly not stopping her from covering her pictures. She is no longer doing this consistently. Suki was a very introverted kind of enveloper, finding large groups difficult to cope with and needed constant reassurance. She clung to the routine and had a tendency to use the same phrases daily, almost creating her own conventions within the existing nursery routine. She reinforced her sense of security by repeating verbally new concepts and ideas at least twice before embarking on a task.

She still needs reassurance, but Suki has managed with sympathetic support to engage in activities that are not particularly enveloping. She still talks about the activity repeatedly before doing it, then after doing it, listing her successes.

Steadily she has become able to access activities freely without necessarily needing these commentaries to buttress her confidence, though she still enjoys reporting successes to adults. She is now a well-rounded child, still with a strong enveloping schema but not hampered by it. In fact she takes initiative, such as in welcoming visitors to the nursery, quizzing them about who they are and the reason for their visit. She delights in being acknowledged by all the people around her.

We have increasingly and unexpectedly found that our approach has been particularly successful in supporting children with autism. We have been able to link up some of their obsessional behaviour or special interests with schematic play and, as we have done with all other children, we have been able to encourage children with autistic spectrum disorders to function 'out of their box' by experiencing different learning patterns, and accessing schematic activities which do not come naturally to them.

Again! Again!

Nicholas had strong rotational and connecting schemas. He sustained play within these two schemas and was not impressed, one week, when the resources and equipment were set up for the enveloping schema. For instance there were a variety of tunnels outside. He watched for quite a while as some children went through the tunnels, but showed no interest in doing it himself. There were several children inside one tunnel, and at this point, Nicholas decided (being a rotator) to roll the tunnel. This brought a lot of giggling from the children, which encouraged him to carry on. After a while, he could not resist going inside the tunnel to experience the fun himself, at which point an adult, then other children took over the rolling. This type of play continued for the rest of the week focusing Nicholas's interest in other types of schematic play, which has continued to this day.

Hardeep arrived at nursery with a strong trajectory schema (focusing on horizontal movements). His constant interest was to kick a ball, often out of the nursery grounds. He would be very lost without a ball and if he could not find one, he would run around seemingly aimlessly without stopping at any activity.

We worked to help him gain precision in his kicking, since the ball often ended up in neighbouring gardens or worse on a major road, which could be dangerous to passing vehicles and where the ball certainly could not be retrieved.

Other forms of target play were incorporated through other schema - balls and other objects going through tunnels (enveloping), balls made out of play dough or clay (rotational). Steadily Hardeep spent a little longer at activities and became more involved in them. He widened his interest to such a point that, after a few months, we realised that he no longer required a ball, although his trajectory instinct still expressed itself through climbing, jumping, making and painting lines. He did return to kicking balls at a later stage, but vertically rather than horizontally. Balls usually ended on top of the nursery roof, and after the loss of a few balls we asked him to solve the problem. He continued to kick vertically without aiming for the roof, creating targets on a tall side wall of the nursery, which fulfilled his needs and prompted many other children to have a go too.

Focusing on schemas has proved to be an effective, accurate and useful diagnostic tool, as well as helping us to find ways to move children's learning forward.

The breadth of children's learning is not haphazard or purely dependent on adults' ideas. It gains a strong structure on which learning can be scaffolded and given direction while still allowing flexibility. Scaffolded learning provides a working structure to support the individual, much like scaffolding does when erecting a building. Each stage relies on previous steps, while providing a strong foundation with opportunities to practise, revisit and link with other knowledge and prior experience. Scaffolding learning enables both the learner and the practitioner to clarify direction, purpose and expectation as well as channelling energy. It is flexible because at each stage you can evaluate, move forward, change direction and meet the needs of each individual, adapting to their interest, pace and ability as well as applying learning to context. As Bruner says:

> *'Learning is figuring out how to use what you already know in order to go beyond what you currently think.'*   *Jerome Bruner*

The use of schemas certainly brought consistency to our short-term planning. It also made us reflect on the schematic strength of different activities and resources. It gave adults the confidence to analyse what was involved in each activity, its objective and ways to exploit the activities to enhance and emulate schemas or to diversify and avoid restrictions. For us, it was all about channelling opportunities and supplementing existing abilities to improve learning.

Focusing on schemas makes planning more appropriate to the needs of individuals and to refine personalised learning. It allows us and the children to have high expectations, and respond to purposeful challenges. The children have individual and personalised targets which are discussed and decided on as opportunity arises, rather than rigidly for all children. Targets take the approach 'I can … ', children gain a sense of achievement for what they can do rather than focussing on what they cannot do. They are not daunted by any task or by any scale - the sky is the limit, because they know that any suggestion will be taken seriously, discussed and explored. They have learnt that part of the discussion is to assess how realistic and realisable the idea is; they have learnt to ascertain whether we have the resources to create their idea; and finally they have learnt in themaking to review and modify their original intentions, and therefore have an end product which may be different from their original idea and usually an improved product from the original thought.

> We (children and adults) had built a Noah's Ark outside with existing resources, mainly an A frame covered with a tarpaulin for the habitable area, some ropes and tyres to mark the shape of the ark, some milk crates to form the front of the ark and to support the helm, a flag pole and a board for the ramp. During a reviewing and planning session with a group of children, one of the children, Ernesto, suggested turning the ark into a pirate ship, using a construction set. The adult pointed out that nearly all the set had already been used in the animal hospital the children had previously built indoors. Ernesto suggested that it could be taken apart to allow for the construction of the ship. However, after discussing with the adult, he understood that it could not happen straight away and he accepted this. The group then agreed to take the hospital down and that they would need to wait for another week before having the resources to pursue the pirate ship project.

An unexpected benefit of using schemas to structure our short-term, child-led planning was that such an approach had a direct impact on the way we address adult-led planning. We have come to realise that our knowledge and understanding of schemas influenced all aspects of our planning as it has permanently changed the way we think and reflect on the children's learning and experiences.

The questions remaining

We started with a question:

How much can knowing about and using schemas help us in continuing to improve our practice and therefore, children's learning?

We have had a very positive outcome in the way it has helped us diagnose, observe and plan. As in any pedagogical development and research, answers to our original question have unearthed many more other questions. It is exciting to try and find ways to answer these questions.

Within our own study, for instance, it appears that most, if not all, rotators are boys. Is this something that could be generalised?

We also found that the majority of connectors were also lateral thinkers. We would like to expand on this. Indeed it begs the question:

Are all lateral thinkers, connectors? We have already found that quite a few rotators are also lateral thinkers. How does this fit in?

We would also like to explore further some of the connections that we have found between schemas and autism.

> *Could this knowledge of a possible connection between schema behaviour and autism help in supporting people with autism?*

We have started to put in place ways of investigating how much influence there is from the schemas and learning styles of significant adults in generating children's dominant schemas, particularly from parents/carers and pedagogues. It seems the fundamental questions may be:

> *Are schemas purely innate or is there some element of choice or control? Can schemas be learned, and if they can, can they also be denied?*

Many of these questions would need a wider study than our small nursery was able to provide, although we can still use our observations and experiences to inform our practice. Rosemary Roberts sums up our feelings when she says:

'Recognising and supporting the development of children's patterns of learning, or schemas, leads to high self-esteem.'

Self-esteem is crucial to the well-being that enables children's complete engagement in their learning. The cameos in these pages are just a small sample of what we have had the privilege of experiencing on a daily basis, learning and playing with the children in our setting.

Rosemary Roberts goes on to say:

'Using our knowledge of schemas can also make it much easier to help children develop skills and competence.'

We certainly have had first-hand experience that it does. Indeed, we would put forward the premise that it does not just benefit the children with strong dominant schemas, it enriches the lives and learning of all children by providing significant, and at times very powerful, opportunities for children and adults to learn alongside each other in a positive and trusting atmosphere.

'Everybody needs the feeling that they are accepted, understood and valued. The recognition and acceptance by adults of children's schematic patterns contributes to these feelings in children. Schemas are at the heart of children's individuality, and so to recognise and support them appropriately is to recognise and support the child on a very fundamental level.'

Reference

Roberts, Rosemary. (2002) Self-Esteem and Early Learning; Paul Chapman

Again! Again!

Examples of planning and observation schedules

Observations

We observe six children every day, as shown in the schedule below. All staff are involved in the observations, recording their comments on 'Post it' notes. These observations go into key group files and are used to plan personalised learning programmes and to inform our short-term, weekly planning. They are also a focus of discussions between staff.

Observation: Key groups: g - green o - orange y - yellow					
	Monday	Tuesday	Wednesday	Thursday	Friday
AM	g - Anjuh o - Brahim y - Ignaw	Michal Sasha Saseeyah	Charlie Max Emile	Benjamin Adam Ella J	Tara Myles Daisy
PM	g - Onri o - Natasha y - Summayyah	Evie Pow Shyal	Kayleigh Lee C Mohammed	Daniel Ysuf Zoe	James Rohit Sophia

Fairies and Elves w/c 2nd June 08 (weekly planner)

| | Leonie/Paul | Gemma/Kerry | Gemma/Leonie | Liz/Paul | Offsite |
	Monday	Tuesday	Wednesday	Thursday	Friday
PSE		Story; Sleeping Beauty (K) 1e - have a positive approach to activities and events			Beeston (Adult led) 3e - Demonstrate flexibility and adapt their behaviours to different events, social situations and changes in routine
CLL	Introductions, the theme (Adult led) - stories with fairies/elves - watch Peter Pan - attributes of fairies - draw a fairy - Gemma	2e - Use talk to connect ideas, explain what is happening and anticipate what might happen next	Writing a spell (list of words and things going into spell) (Adult led) write on their drawing - Monday - Kerry	Own books - Leonie (Adult led) 6e - Make connections between different parts if their life experiences; 5g - Attempt writing for different purposes using features of different forms such as lists, stories and instructions	
PSRN	DVD Fairies (K) 2c - Are learning to classify				Finish dens, fairy dens (Adult led) 3e - Show interest in shape by sustaining construction activity or by talking about shapes or arrangements
KUW	Planting (Adult led) Kerry 1e - Show curiosity about why things happen	Planting (Adult led) Leonie 1f Show awareness of change	Planting (Adult led) Paul 5e - Show an interest in the world in which they live	Planting (Adult led) Gemma/Fay	Pond dipping (green group first) (Adult led) 1e - Describe and talk about what they see Kerry and Sam
PHYSICAL AND CREATIVE	What to build for next week's imaginative area with quadro (K) 1f - Express and communicate their ideas, thoughts and feelings 3f - Manipulate material to achieve a planned effect Making magic wings and wands (hats?) - Paul (Adult led)				Water paint 2d - Begin to combine movement, materials, media or marks

Numbers indicate EYFS intentions
Additional notes handwritten on reverse of this sheet

Again! Again!

Linking Schema play with Early Years intentions

SCHEMAS	Week beg ... Transporting		Week beg ... Connection		Week beg ... Enveloping	
Games & puzzles	Use number names in play	Hopscotch			Use ideas to solve problems	Games & puzzles
Numbers & calc	Find total in 2 grps by counting	Shop				
Shape, space, meas			Actiys involving eye/hand co-ord	Threading beads		
Small construction	Show character-istics & preferences			Building bricks	Create on large/small scale	Marble run
Large construction	Use language to share creations	Tyres and crates			Begin using more complex sentences	Den building
Small world	Show character-istics & preferences	Train track	Begin to use toys to pretend	Happy town	Interact with peers, take turns	Doll play
Role play					Experiment with ways of moving	Tents & tunnels
Imaginative play				Castle or rocket	Persevere when learning new skill	Castle
Builder's tray				Building bricks		
Exploration	Show interest in why things happen	Cow in canal	Show curiosity & interest ...	tapioca 'frogspawn'		
Investigation			Ask about why things happen...	Pulleys	Use simple tools & techniques	Boxes
ICT	Show interest in ICT	CD-ROM			Sustain attentive listening	Stories on tape
Sound & music			Explore sounds of instruments	Make instruments	Persevere when learning new skill	
Phonics						
Reading		Books on the theme	→			
Workshop	Distinguish between marks they make	Writing	Create 3D structures	Box modelling	Use simple tools & techniques	Use boxes, tape for containers
Fabrics						
Visual arts	Explore & name colours	Water colour & straws	Seek out others to share experiences	Texture prints	Continue to be interested/involved	Candle wax paintings
Graphic						
Malleable	Explore malleable materials	Cornflour		Cutting jelly/grass	Awareness and pride in self	Tubes
Sand	Make-believe by pretending	Tracks			Use language to imagine & create	Washing things
Water	Use words & gesture	Waterway	Display high levels of involvement	Step ladder, guttering, pipes		
Motor skills (gross)	Use body to create movements	Hoops				
Motor skills (fine)			Explore materials by patting etc	Pink dough	Differentiate marks and movements	Writing table, post box
Extra	Seek out others to share experiences	Big cars	Explore materials by patting etc			
Extra						

Using schemas in planning

Again! Again!

Working with other practitioners and settings

Transitions, or changes in a baby's or child's environment happen all the time, as they grow and develop, and as their family or cultural circumstances change. For one baby, this might mean starting at a day nursery at six weeks of age, for another it might be spending time with a grandparent or childminder, for yet another it might be starting in a Reception class at the age of four with no previous experience of out-of-home care. These transitions can be smooth or traumatic, and one element which can smooth transition is information in manageable and useful amounts. Nothing can replace talking together about the individual baby or child, but this conversation should be supported by notes, photos, anecdotes and other information that confirm the conversation.

This comment by Tina Bruce, is a vivid reminder to us of the importance of keeping records and sharing these with the others who will be caring for the individual child:

> *'Record-keeping which attempts to identify the schema, to plot its level, and see how the child uses the environment and responds ... helps to fill in some detail. It is not possible to rescue someone lost in a wood if you do not know where they are.'*
> Tina Bruce

Practitioners have a duty to pass on information to other colleagues about children's schemas, as well as their sleeping and eating preferences, their friends, their worries and concerns. Records should ensure that wherever and whenever the child moves, the necessary information is available to support these individual interests and needs. Children's' progress, achievement and attainment will all be improved if knowledge of current schemas informs the ongoing provision for children.

Sometimes practitioners in the new setting are not aware of or used to observing schemas, and in this case some information, an offer of a short staff meeting or a presentation using photos or video of children's play could be the start of a useful dialogue between local settings. Such presentations could become ongoing part of local networks, built into the annual programme and based on the work of individual settings and practitioners, or shared sessions on planning and record keeping systems. This is often the most powerful way of exploring and extending good practice.

How practitioners pass on information to other colleagues about children's interests, what motivates them and their current schemas is important and should involve parents and children. *Continuing the Learning Journey* (DfES, 2005) discusses the importance of maintaining partnerships with parents during transition from Reception to Year 1 in schools, and describes this as:

> *'Two-way flow of information; what happens at school is reinforced at home and vice versa.'*   Continuing the Learning Journey

Working with Parents

The research carried out by Chris Athey, Tina Bruce, Cathy Nutbrown and PEEP all involved parents as co-researchers by valuing the observations they made of their children's schemas in action at home.

Pen Green Children's Centre in Corby has led the way in promoting such work with parents by training and encouraging parents to take photos and make diaries, audiotapes and videos of how their children play at home, and using these alongside observations made of children's learning in the nursery. The staff team at Pen Green value parents' contributions to their children's learning and recognise that practitioners need information about children's' interests outside the nursery setting if they are to provide children with a supportive stimulating and challenging curriculum. Cameras were provided by the nursery for the parents to do this crucial partnership work.

> *'Parents and staff began to see themselves as co-educators, co-constructing an appropriate curriculum to meet the cognitive affective needs of every child.'*   Margy Whalley

The development of the Pen Green Feedback Loop, resulting from partnership work with families, now links all the important people in each child's life, giving feedback on what currently interests and motivates the child and how and what they are learning at home, at nursery, or pre-school. You can find out more about this project on the CD-ROM from the EYFS Pack.

In *Involving Parents in their Children's Learning*, Cath Arnold, currently head of Pen Green Nursery describes some first-rate ways of sharing observations and ideas about children with parents, and shows how sharing the language of schemas with parents is an important step in helping them to understand the EYFS and its contents, particularly when discussing aspects of Learning and Development. Talking to parents about repeated play patterns encourages them to share the detailed and personal information and insight they have into their child's learning.

> *'One very vivid and immediate way of sharing knowledge with parents about their children is to use photographs.'*   Cath Arnold

Again! Again!   —

Cath Arnold suggests that if practitioners take photographs of children and their schemas, then parents, who may be struggling to relate to or provide support for their children, will have a visual aid to empower them to become more involved in understanding their child's learning. In this way, not only is a dialogue created between parent and practitioner but an atmosphere of mutual respect can result, and as the relationship develops, parents have a better insight into their children's' play and explorations both at home and in the nursery. Practitioners should be encouraged to be open with parents, asking them for a range of information about a child's interests, building a firm foundation for a genuine working partnership.

Schema workshops are another way of helping parents to understand the nature of their children's behaviour and learning. These workshops can inform parents about schemas, the importance of active learning, and how parents can begin to support and extend play at home. Photographs and examples of observations of schemas in action can be keys to understanding.

Parents and professionals can help children separately or they can work together to the greater benefit of children.'   Chris Athey

Knowledge of schemas will help parents to describe their children's play and explorations in different ways, enabling them to focus on their children's actions in a more informed way, and helping them to develop strategies for supporting and redirecting play.

'Educators need to move on from identifying patterns of behaviour to explaining to parents how they use such knowledge of schemas to plan and provide learning.'   Cathy Nutbrown

Both parents and practitioners can have a powerful influence on the lives and learning of babies and young children. However, babies and young children learn most of their values, culture and beliefs from their parents. Practitioners have two client groups - the children being the primary one and the parents being the secondary one - but it is not possible to work with a child effectively in isolation from its parents. Practitioners need to recognise parents as partners in their children's learning and engage them in the learning process, helping them to value their own part in their child's future.

References

Arnold, C. (2003) <u>Child Development and Learning 0-5: Observing Harry</u>; Open University Press, Maidenhead.

Bruce, Tina. (1996) <u>Early Childhood Education</u>; Hodder & Stoughton

DfES. (2005) <u>Continuing the Learning Journey</u>; DfES

Whalley, Margy. (1994) <u>Learning to be Strong, Setting up a neighbourhood service for under-fives and their families</u>, Hodder & Stoughton

Whalley, Margy and the Pen Green Team. (2001) <u>Involving Parents in their Children's Learning</u>; Paul Chapman

Athey, Chris. (1990) <u>Extending Thought in Young Children</u>; Paul Chapman

Nutbrown, Cathy. (1999) <u>Threads of Thinking</u>; Paul Chapman

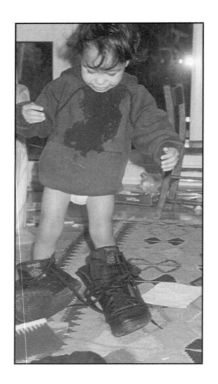

BIBLIOGRAPHY

Arnold, C. (2003) Child Development and Learning 0-5; Observing Harry. Open University Press, Maidenhead.

Arnold, C. Child Development and Learning 2-5 Years; Georgia's Story. Paul Chapman.

Athey, C. (1990) Extending Thoughts in Young Children; Paul Chapman

Bayley, Ros and Featherstone Sally. (2006) Foundations for Independence; Featherstone Education

Bayley, Ros and Featherstone, Sally. (2003) Smooth Transitions; Featherstone Education

Brainerd Charles. (1978) Piaget's Theory of Intelligence; Prentice-Hall

Bruce, Tina. (1996) Helping Young Children to Play; Hodder & Stoughton

Bruce, T. (2001) Learning Through Play: Babies, Toddlers and the Foundation Years; Hodder & Stoughton

Bruce, T. (1991) A Time to Play; Hodder & Stoughton

Bruce, T. (1987) Early Childhood Education; Hodder & Stoughton

Bruce Tina and Meggitt Carolyn. (2002) Child Care & Education; Hodder and & Stoughton

Bruner; Jerome. (1967) Towards a Theory of Instruction; Harvard University

Bruner, J. (1986) Actual Minds, Possible Worlds; Harvard University Press

David, T. Advances in Applied Early Childhood Education. Vol. 1. Promoting Evidence-based Practice in Early Childhood Education; Research and its Implications London, JAL

Davis, Mollie. (1995) Helping Children to Learn Through a Movement Perspective; Hodder & Stoughton

Davis, Mollie. (2003) Movement and Dance in Early Childhood; Paul Chapman

DfES/QCA; (2000) Curriculum Guidance for the Foundation Stage; QCA

DfES/Surestart (2003) Birth to Three Matters: A Framework to Support Children in the Earliest Years; SureStart/DfES

DfES; (2005) Continuing the Learning Journey; DfES

DfES; (2006) Early Years Foundation Stage Consultation; DfES

DfES; (2007/2008) Early Years Foundation Stage; DfES

Drummond, Mary Jane. (1993) Assessing Children's Learning; David Fulton

Duffy, Bernadette. (1998) Supporting Creativity and Imagination in the Early Years; Open University Press

Evangelou, M. and Sylva, K. (2003) PEEP The Effects of the Early Education Partnership on Children's Developmental Progress, Research Report 489.

Fisher, E. (ed) (1984) Language Development; Croom Helm/Open University

Gopnik, A. Meltzoff, A. and Kuhl, P. (1999) How Babies Think; Phoenix

Gura, P. and Bruce, T. (1992) Exploring Learning, Young Children and Blockplay; Hodder and Stoughton.

Gross, Richard. (2005) Psychology: The Science of Mind and Behaviour: Hodder & Stoughton

Holland, Penny. (2003) We Don't Play with Guns Here; War, weapons and superhero play in the early years; Open University Press

Hutchin, Vicky. (2003) Observing and Assessing for the Foundation Stage Profile; Hodder Murray

Johnston, Jane. (2005) Early explorations in science: Exploring primary science and technology education; Open University Press

Kilton, Neil. (1994) The Excellence of Play; Open University Press

Leach, Penelope. (1997) Baby & Child: From Birth to Age Five; Penguin

Lindon, Jennie. (2001) Understanding Children's Play; Nelson Thornes

Manning-Morton, J. and Thorp, M. (2001) Key Times for Developing High Quality Provision for Children Under Three Years Old; Camden Early Years Under Three Development Group

Manning-Morton, J. and Thorp, M. (2003) Key Times for Play; The First Three Years; Open University Press

Matthews, John. (2003) Drawing and Painting; Children and Visual Representation; Paul Chapman

Meade, Anne with Cubey, Pam. (1995) Thinking Children; New Zealand Council for Educational Research

Meade, Anne. One Hundred Billion Neurons: How do they become organised?; Advances in Applied Early Childhood Education. Vol. 1. Promoting Evidence-based Practice in Early Childhood Education.

Minett, Pamela. (1985) Child Care & Development; John Murray

Murray, Lynne and Andrews, Liz. (2000) The Social Baby, Understanding Babies' Communication from Birth; The Children's Project

Nutbrown, C. (1999) Threads of Thinking: Young Children Learning and the Role of Early Education; Paul Chapman

Ouvry, Marjorie. (2005) Exercising Muscles and Minds: Outdoor play and the early years curriculum; National Children's Bureau

Papert, Seymour. (1980) Mind Storms: Children, Computers, and Powerful ideas; Harvester Press, in Early Childhood Education; Hodder Arnold

Piaget, J. (1962) Play, Dreams and Imitations in Childhood; Routledge & Kegan Paul

Piaget J. (1980) Adaptation and Intelligence; University of Chicago Press

Post J and Hohmann M. (2000) Tender Care and Early Learning, Supporting Families and Toddlers in Childcare Settings; High/Scope Press

Rodd; Jillian. (1994) Leadership in Early Years; Pathway to Professionalism; Open

University Press

Roberts, Rosemary. (2006) <u>Self-Esteem and Early Learning</u>; Key People from Birth to School; Paul Chapman

Selleck, Dorothy and Griffin, S. (2006) <u>Quality for the Under Threes in Contemporary Issues in the Early Years</u>; Sage

Sheridan, M. (1975) <u>Children's Developmental Progress from Birth to Five Years</u>; NFER.

Shore, R. (1997) <u>Rethinking the Brain</u>, New insights into Early Development; Families and Work Institute

Siraj-Blatchford, Iram. and Sylva, Kathy (2002) <u>Researching Effective Pedagogy in Early Years</u>; DfES

Tassoni, Penny. and Tucker, Karen. (2000) <u>Planning Play and the Early Years</u>; Heinemann Educational

Vygotsky, L. (1978) <u>Minds in Society</u>; Harvard University Press

Vygotsky, L. (1986) <u>Thought and Language</u>; MIT Press

Weikart, D. (2001) <u>Early Childhood Education</u>: Need and Opportunity. Unesco Publishing

Whalley, Margy. (1994) <u>Learning to be Strong</u>, Setting up a neighbourhood service for under-fives and their families; Hodder & Stoughton

Whalley, Margy. and the Pen Green Team. (2001) <u>Involving Parents in their Children's Learning</u>; Paul Chapman/Sage

Whitehead, Marion. (2002) <u>Developing Language and Literacy with Young Children</u>; Paul Chapman

'Child-centred programmes with ready access to materials are important, because they allow children to construct a lot of knowledge about schemas for themselves ...

... the materials' enrichment does appear to be a significant factor, especially since the additional materials were carefully chosen to fit the children's intellectual fascinations and not because they were attractive to adults.'

Thinking Children; Anne Meade and Pam Cubey

Like Bees, not Butterflies

Child-initiated learning

Why is it that, when children play, some behave like butterflies, flitting around among the flowers of the activities we offer, landing for a moment before moving on to the next attractive flower, while others behave with the single minded concentration of bees?

As children grow and learn, they acquire skills through play and practical activities. This recently acquired learning is tenuous and is secured through practice, repeating the skills in different contexts, with different resources and with different people. Only then will learning be 'hard wired' for life. It is now evident that where children are able to select resources, play companions and activities for themselves, they can practice emerging skills, knowledge and concepts by selecting the resources they need and using them in ways which are unique to them.

This book, written by a group of experts in early years practice, explores the place and purpose of child initiated learning in high quality early years practice.

Edited by Sally & Phill Featherstone

Contributions by	Jane Cole	Theodora Papatheodorou
Ros Bayley	**Pam Lafferty**	**Linda Pound**
Helen Bilton	**Jennie Lindon**	**Wendy Scott**
Lynn Broadbent	**Janet Moyles**	**Judith Stevens**
Jan Dubiel	**Sue Palmer**	

£16.99   ISBN 978-1-906029-76-0

Child-initiated learning is a key feature of the new Early Years Foundation Stage, which will be implemented in September 2008. This book will provide support, encouragement and ideas for practitioners, students, their managers and advisers as they take on one of the next challenges in early years development.

To see the full range of Featherstone books visit www.acblack.com/featherstone

L is for Sheep

Getting ready for phonics

Everyone agrees that an understanding of phonics is essential to cracking the code for reading.

In **L is for Sheep** fourteen early years experts bring balance and common sense to the discussion of phonics. Part 1 consists on articles on where phonological awareness fits into what we know about the development of young children. Part 2 contains practical suggestions and guidance on getting children ready for phonics and starting on reading.

L is for Sheep
– getting ready for phonics

Ros Bayley, Helen Bilton, Lynn Broadbent,
Marion Dowling, Margaret Edgington, Janet Evans,
Judith Harries, Jennie Lindon, Janet Moyles, Linda Pound,
Kym Scott, Judith Stevens, Penny Tassoni
Edited by Sally Featherstone

Edited by Sally Featherstone

Contributions by
Ros Bayley
Helen Bilton
Lynn Broadbent
Marion Dowling

Margaret Edgington
Janet Evans
Judith Harries
Jennie Lindon
Janet Moyles

Linda Pound
Kym Scott
Judith Stevens
Penny Tassoni

'A treasure chest of reassurance, research evidence and really practical advice... a lively text that will enable you to make sense of the current debates, but also to reach your own principled conclusions as to the best ways to foster early literacy.'

Mary Jane Drummond

£16.99   ISBN 978-1-905019-63-2

To see the full range of Featherstone books visit www.acblack.com/featherstone